Memoirs of Successful Women

COMPILED BY
ANNIE GIBBINS

Copyright © 2023 by Annie Gibbins

All rights reserved. No part of this book may be used or reproduced by any means, graphic, electronic, or mechanical, including photocopying, recording, taping or by any information storage retrieval system without the written permission of the copyright owner except in the case of brief quotations embodied in critical articles and reviews. Because of the dynamic nature of the Internet, any web addresses or links contained in this book may have changed since publication and may no longer be valid. The views expressed in this work are solely those of the author and do not necessarily reflect the views of the publisher and the publisher hereby disclaims any responsibility for them.

Annie Gibbins / Women's Biz Publishing
New South Wales, Australia
www.womensbizpublishing.com

Book Layout © 2023 womensbizpublishing.com

Heart Warrior/ Annie Gibbins -- 1st ed.
978-1-922969-06-4

womensbizglobal.com

COMPILED BY ANNIE GIBBINS

Dedication

The women of the world who dare to rise and forge
their path towards success.

COMPILED BY ANNIE GIBBINS

CONTENTS

ANNIE GIBBINS 1
HEIDI DUGAN 9
SUZY MICHAEL 15
SHELLI BRUNSWICK 28
PATRICIA GROVER 33
LAYNE BEACHLEY 47
REV.JOSLYN FARRAY PIERRE 55
MARLEY MAJCHER 66
KEZ WICKHAM ST GEORGE 75
POOJA BHATIA 87
SWATI TYAGI 95
ANNIE GIBBINS 114

DEFINE SUCCESS ON YOUR TERMS

ANNIE GIBBINS

> "I've come to believe that each of us has a personal calling that's as unique as a fingerprint – and that the best way to succeed, is to discover what you love and then find a way to offer it to others in the form of service, working hard, and also allowing the energy of the universe to lead you." — Oprah Winfrey

I travel on a lot of planes. I sit in a lot of airport lounges and Uber rides, to and from various hotels around Australia. So, it's unsurprising that I have a lot of 'planning' time. I would go as far to say that some of my best ideas have been created 30,000 feet in the air. It's crazy really, that nowadays life can be led almost anywhere.

During one of my most recent flights, I was working on a keynote speech for an awards event. As I was tapping away on my fold-down tray table, with a packet of pretzels and a mini bottle of prosecco neatly tucked against my laptop, I was thinking about the true meaning of 'success'. What became increasingly apparent was that as I began listing my own successes to date, there was no one true meaning behind the word 'success'.

Sure, the front-runners in the success measurement leader board can be wealth, riches, marital status, home ownership and career stature. You could say success in these terms is fairly obvious and standard. But really, who wants standard success? Don't get me wrong, money might not necessarily make us happy, but funds in the bank can certainly make life a little easier. For many leaders, success can be reflected in a job title or company shares. A long marriage can certainly make a couple feel successful, however for others, marriage simply isn't even on their radar.

As I sipped my prosecco out of a plastic cup (hello airlines, not eco-cool at all), I was inspired to think beyond 'ordinary'. As many of my friends, family and clients will testify, "there is nothing ordinary about Annie Gibbins". I am a curious, adventurous soul-seeker, on an unwavering mission to leave a lasting legacy in this world. Truly, as I was framing my interpretation of success, and how we can all achieve whatever we want, how we want it and when, my fingers couldn't type fast enough, Side note, doing the right thing, doesn't always feel right at the time. Remember the comfort zone, but also remember we don't want to sit in it forever.

So, why now? Why this book?

As the successful podcast host of my long running show, 'Memoirs of Successful Women', I have interviewed over one hundred and fifty women, who have been successful, on their terms. These women have been business leaders, CEOs, authors, teachers, inventors, mothers, creatives, innovators, philanthropists, social conscious disruptors, mothers, actors, healers, doctors, astrophysicists and so much more.

As a published author, and now hedging my own independent Publishing House, it made complete and utter sense to me, to share the stories of others. The science behind the power of storytelling is fierce and has the ability to radicalise dormant thinking, unearth new ideas and connect people together, in a world that at times, is massively disconnected.

If I was to reflect on my memories, I would say that some of my happiest moments have been in the company of women. Our gatherings haven't always been glam social occasions, global conferences, or fancy cocktail hours. The simplicity of sipping on a chai tea with a close friend, can satiate me for days. When we share our experiences, big or small, we ignite a sense of empathy and relatability. We feel that we belong.

Beneath the bravado and many masks, we wear as women, is a desire to move as a tribe. Ancient rituals and historical communities functioned because they worked as one. As they say, 'it takes a village to raise a child'. And it's so true. Women need women; they need support, empowerment, care and guidance. To thrive as individuals, we must interweave as a family, some long distance and some, a little closer to home.

What would you be glad you did--even if you failed? Talk about your failures without apologising. It's not about "what can I accomplish?" but "what do I want to accomplish?"

Paradigm shift.

Connection is why we're here; it is what gives purpose and meaning to our lives. To me, a leader is someone who holds her, or himself, accountable for finding potential in people and processes. Authenticity is a collection of choices that we must make every day. I don't have to chase extraordinary moments to find happiness-it's right in front of me if I'm paying attention and practicing gratitude." – **Brené Brown**

I often ask myself, have we overcomplicated success, or have we been too simple with the ways and days towards a successful life? Take my friend Alissa for example. She worked in a corporate job for ten years, had an office overlooking Sydney harbour, and lived a stone's throw distance from the beach. Her evenings were spent wining and dining in elite city bars and schmoozing with the high-flyers of the metropolitan mecca.

On weekends Alissa would arm herself with a yoga mat, green juice, and a beach bag packed with her favourite books and iPod shuffle list. From the outside, women wanted to be her, men wanted to be with her.

She had everything... or did she?

Not long after the pandemic, still working from home, and with only a few friends that she called, 'close', she realised deep down, she was desperately unhappy. Alissa was covering her loneliness with being busy, and despite a decent pay-packet, her life felt empty, and devoid of true meaning and substance. So, she quit it all. She handed in her notice, sold her belongings and vacated her beachside pad. With a one-way ticket to Europe, Alissa went on her own discovery of success.

Sure, additional funds in the bank helped, but what she needed versus her bank balance, were worlds apart. She didn't need a fancy life – she needed connection. She needed to speak from her heart, simplify her schedule, and discover her purpose. As it turns out, Alissa now teaches yoga from her patio, is a freelance consultant, and reads books from morning to night. Her Sunday mornings are spent sipping tea in the garden and calling her family, whom she had become so distant from before.

Alissa thought she knew what success was. However, a slick apartment, with the trendiest interiors didn't welcome her home at night. Her resume didn't wake up with her on a Sunday morning. Her avid dating ritual didn't deliver her love.

After chatting with Alissa last week, for the first time, I saw a woman with less strain across her brow, bright eyes, and a calmer energy. Sure, she still has bad days, because after all, Alissa is human. Aren't we all?

But what she does with the bad days is crucial. She doesn't distract herself by creating new lists or making plans to fill the voids of a quieter life. Doing nothing is good for us. Peace and serenity are priceless and as we know, the one thing we can never gain back, is time.

Time to reflect and question our success.

You may choose to write a book that you've been putting off for years or plan a business venture that has sat on the back burner. You may choose to book that trip that you've had pinned underneath your fridge magnet or ask your crush out on a dinner date. You may choose to enrol in an evening class or an online course.

You may choose to take your family out for a meal, instead of watching TV. You may choose to make a family, where your career once took precedence, or you may choose to return to work, after raising your family alone. You may even choose to do nothing, because doing nothing is a choice. You may choose to speak up at the next work meeting, where you felt too nervous to before, or apply for the promotion that everyone comments, "is a waste of your time, you'll never land the job".

Well, you can land the job, because that's what I have done for all my career.

I've seen, clutched, conquered, and delivered.

So, the big, million-dollar question is, "can we have it all?"

Simply, yes.

But we may not have it 'all' at the same time.

And that's okay.

Success shouldn't be consumed like an oversized meal when you're hungry. Success should be devoured like a three-course meal at Christmas, or a rare delicacy that you're experiencing for the first time.

Success is the perfect complement to contentment.

Contentment is enough, and that's a big win in my eyes. Ultimately, success starts the moment you choose you. Not in a selfish or self-indulgent version of your successful self, but the parts of you that you've abandoned over time.

Detangling, and deconstructing ourselves first, means we can truly define what success means and feels to us, on a spiritual, emotional and physical level. As they say, 'comparison is the thief of happiness', so I encourage you to stop scrolling, looking for the life you want. Instead, turn your phone onto flight mode and sink deeper within. You know the answers – you *have* the answers, so use them wisely.

This is why I am bringing this book to your hot little hands. Throughout this anthology, you will read stories from women who have experienced loss, adversity, breakthroughs, and hard times. Their stories, rooted in deep heartiness and humanity, have been uncovered and discovered by a will to live more, be more and feel more.

As you turn the pages, you will be inspired to think about what happiness and success means to you. You will be invited to define success in your own terms, as each author guides you through their milestone moments. We live in a big and very small world. Ironically, I live half my life in the air (Okay, slight exaggeration), but I do spend a lot of my days transiting across the world, usually with my gorgeous husband James, by my side. We love to travel and the love we have for each other also remains strong.

Ah love, the engine room to a happy life.

So, despite always being on the move, I feel more connected than ever. I am a tech-fiend who maximises on many digital platforms to stay close to loved ones. I can't tell you how many applications I currently have on my desktop, most of which are communication tools to keep my business pumping. I have created and designed my life to never be too far from what success has to offer.

I make it happen. I engineer my future because I know what I want. My vision is clear, optimistic, energised, and versatile and I am always, always, open to change.

I hope throughout reading this book, you will find the answers you've been looking for, feel excited for what's to come and ultimately, feel a sense of absolute belonging.

You sister have got this.

"I love to see a young girl go out and grab the world by the lapels. Life's a bitch. You've got to go out and kick ass."

— *Maya Angelou*

BECOMING AN INFLUENCER: FROM CHINA TO AUSTRALIA, AND BEYOND

HEIDI DUGAN

My journey has been an incredible rollercoaster of twists and turns, taking me to places I never thought possible. If you had told my younger self that I would become an Australian woman making a significant impact on the business landscape in China, I would have dismissed it as a far-fetched dream. But here I stand today, having spent nearly three decades living and working in China, building a public presence that connects me with governments and multinational corporations, while amassing a following and TV viewership of over six million.

It all began with a gentle nudge from my parents, for which I'm eternally grateful. Their support, along with that of my family, children, and friends, has been my bedrock, empowering me to navigate the highs and lows of building a successful profile and businesses that I'm immensely proud of.

Reflecting on this incredible journey, I can't help but wonder how it all started and which decisions and actions set me on this path. In 1996, I stumbled upon a course offered by an Australian University The Royal Institute of Technology, in Wuhan, a place that was nowhere on my radar back then. At the time, I aspired to pursue an acting career and had my sights set on the UK and the US. However, my acting teacher imparted a valuable lesson, insisting that "to be a great actor, you need to get out and experience life." Little did she know that her words would redirect my entire trajectory. China, as it turned out, became the perfect canvas for me to paint the life of my dreams.

With my bags packed and a visa in hand, I took a leap of faith, boarding a plane bound for China just two weeks later.

From the moment I touched down on Chinese soil, opportunities unfurled before me like an endless tapestry. Each time I contemplated saying "yes" to a new opportunity, I reminded myself, "Well, I've come this far; I might as well give this a try too."

Living in China taught me two invaluable lessons. Firstly, as a foreigner, I was never expected to conform. I looked different, acted differently, and, at that time, didn't speak the same language. This uniqueness became my strength. I came to understand that others' judgments of me were just that—their judgments, and their judgements did not define me. This realisation liberated me from the fear of failure, embarrassment, or the need to please others. I was unmistakably different, and that was perfectly okay.

Embracing my uniqueness led me to explore the question, "Who am I?" The more I asked myself, the clearer my values, aspirations, and the kind of person I wanted to become became. Armed with these insights, I made decision after decision that propelled me from where I was then to where I am now.

One significant turning point came when I was asked to groom the Chinese news hosts and teach them how to present on TV in English. This led to the TV station asking me to be a guest host on one of the other shows. They eventually obtained the license to have foreign TV hosts, and within days, my show "You Are the Chef" was created. I became the first foreign TV host to have her own show in China, a show that has now achieved cult status, airing daily morning, midday, and evening, attracting over 6 million viewers each time.

I did the show my way, even hosting it until I was eight months pregnant, a feat that had never been done before. After giving birth to both my daughter and son, I made a groundbreaking decision to bring them on the TV with me, letting my followers see the real me and understand more about who I was. To this day, people still comment on the show where I introduced my babies.

With the increasing popularity of the show, the more people became fascinated with my life. Magazines, newspapers, and other TV shows began reaching out to interview me about my story, how I work, stay fit and healthy, and raise two children. In China, it wasn't just about what I did, but how I did it that intrigued people.

One exhilarating experience was transitioning to the shopping channel, where I was responsible for live selling to people on the other end of the camera. The adrenaline that pumped through my veins during these live broadcasts was incredible. I had to juggle live data analytics, product knowledge, and sales pitch while watching sales skyrocket in real-time. It was a thrilling and intense experience.

Despite living a public lifestyle, many in the media industry will tell you that a career in television is something you learn to appreciate year-by-year. Hitting twenty years in the business is truly a great success and one that I've never taken for granted. The exposure to consumer demographics, sales analytics, presenting, and product knowledge offered me insight into business in so many ways that a boardroom cannot provide.

China has always been ahead in identifying market shifts, and being privy to this gave me a significant business advantage. Witnessing how fast markets can pivot and subsequently affect brands was a front-row seat to understanding market dynamics. Acting with urgency, I knew I needed to build my brand and social media presence to capture a market before my competitors did. This proactive approach contributed to my success today.

Starting a new life in a foreign country isn't easy. In my case, the Chinese business community and the consumer gave me a chance, recognizing the value I brought with my Western knowledge of how to communicate products differently. By bridging the gap between Western and Eastern markets, I offered a fresh perspective to Chinese consumers, and they loved it.

Before I knew it, I was considered a 'woman to watch,' a title I've never taken lightly. Even in the early days, despite the nerves of presenting live on TV, I knew I was being watched—not only by consumers but also by some of the biggest brands out there. Every day, I was selling products and representing my brand, and it paid off.

Regardless of the industry, reputation is everything and it follows you everywhere. Personally, I believe the golden quality is authenticity, which is something that you can truly develop over the years into something magnificent. In many ways, I think that's why I've had such incredible success in China. I've always remained true to myself and the person I wanted to be, and I continue to be grateful to my family, my friends and all the people that have had a part at shaping me. I'm grateful for the opportunities this country has given me, and that gratitude continually presents itself as authentic which only comes from truly knowing yourself.

As someone who has traversed the uncharted territories of entrepreneurship, television, and cross-cultural communication, I am more than just a witness to success—I am an expert who's dedicated to sharing my wealth of experiences. My journey has been a remarkable odyssey, shaped by relentless determination, creative thinking, and the courage to embrace uniqueness. From creating thriving businesses to crafting a persona of influence, I've garnered insights that I'm passionate about imparting. My goal is to empower individuals like you with the knowledge and strategies necessary to navigate the complexities of business, harness the power of authenticity, and become influential leaders in your own right.

Let me spill the beans on why I'm so excited to share my incredible journey with you. It's not to boast, but to show you what is possible. I've spent years zigzagging through the world of entrepreneurship, television, marketing, building an IP and cross-cultural adventures, and let me tell you, it's been a wild ride. But here's the juicy part—I'm not just here to chat about my journey; I'm your go-to expert, ready to show you the real deal on how to make it in business, build an influential persona, and so much more.

I aim to illuminate a path to success, one that transcends borders and empowers you to achieve greatness. Let's embark on this transformative journey together, where I'll equip you with the tools and wisdom needed to conquer challenges, seize opportunities, and emerge as a force to be reckoned with in your endeavors.

Think of me as your friendly guide, someone who's been through the trenches and wants to spill all the secrets. From crafting successful businesses to carving out a unique and influential persona, I've got a treasure trove of wisdom to share and will show you all the "behind the scenes" things I do.

My mission?

To help you navigate the twists and turns, overcome obstacles, and become a powerhouse in your own right. So, let's dive into this adventure together. I'll arm you with the know-how and savvy to tackle challenges, seize opportunities, and shine bright in whatever you set your sights on.

Ready to embark on this journey?

I sure am

"It took me quite a long time to develop a voice, and now that I have it, I am not going to be silent."

— Madeleine Albright

WITH THE RIGHT MINDSET SHE CAN ACHIEVE ANYTHING HER HEART DESIRES

SUZY MICHAEL

Who we are, is defined for us from the moment we are born. We have no say in what type of family we are born into, and what we are taught in our first ten to twelve years of life. I was born into a religious family. My grandfather was a priest, and my mother was the priest's daughter. Our family unit revolved around church. I was raised in a tight-knit Christian family with both sets of parents and grandparents, aunties, uncles, cousins, and extended cousins.

I was immersed in Sunday School, Choir, Youth Group, as well as fundraising activities, and was always taught the importance of humanity and being Christ-like. One of the first things I was taught in Sunday School was "I can do all things through Christ who strengthens me" (Phil 4:13), and I really believed that. As a young, impressionable, seven-year-old child, I believed.

So, I went about all my usual life activities as a child and teenager, with this verse deeply rooted in my mind and heart. Any challenges that came my way, weren't a problem, I could do them. This verse shaped me and made me who I am today. This verse impacted, and still impacts, my thoughts, my actions, my ambitions, my drive and my why.

That's the defining moment for everyone – to be able to confidently answer the question, "What's my why?"

To get to the root of my 'why', I delved into my childhood years. In life, there are a lot of things beyond our control. What we do have control over is how we react to whatever happens in our lives.

Your reaction will be dependent on your beliefs, your upbringings, and your decisions. It may not be Christ for you, but there is a force, an energy, a bigger hand at play that drives you and makes you who you are: Your mantra, your beliefs, your inner voice.

When I was seven years old, my grandfather asked me, "What did you learn in Sunday school today?" and I answered, "We learned we can do anything through Christ who strengthens us."

He smiled and said, "Never forget that. You can do ANYTHING with Christ's strength and love and guidance."

I remember that at the exact moment I was speaking with him, I felt a 'voice' inside me, a feeling, telling me that I was going to live a successful life.

A feeling of reassurance washed over me, and I felt 'empowered', knowing I was going to be great. I didn't know how; I just had a feeling. And I replied to my grandfather, "Yep…. I will never forget that."

At the time, I didn't know what spirituality was. I thought I knew who God was, who Jesus was, and I didn't think it was God speaking to me. It felt like a force, or some kind of energy, washed over me, giving me the sensation that great accomplishment and success will come my way. All I could hear in my seven-year-old head was, "I am going to do great things for the world."

I wanted to be a journalist, because giving information to the world can, in turn, help the world be a better place.

Another moment I recall is when I was about nine years old. My daily ritual was watching the evening news with my dad. Growing up as a young child, in the eighties, gangs were prevalent, and I would see the murders, rapes, crime and gang activities being regularly reported.

The nightly news was filled with scary stories, tragedies, and terror. In my mind, there was a very dark portrayal of the society I lived in, but I knew it wasn't the real world.

By the time I was 11, I decided I wanted to bring good news to the TV screens. I was determined to show the wider society it wasn't just doom and gloom, and that there were many good news stories that didn't get reported.

That there were incredible people doing charity work and contributing amazing things to society. I knew about these inspiring contributors, because I saw it in action through my church community, which is all I knew at the time.

Yet the gangs and crimes filled up the nightly news and newspapers and were a constant heated topic of discussion. To a young girl living in the 1980's who was always exposed to community, family, love and caring for others, it begged the question in my mind: "What about all the good in the world that is being ignored?"

At that moment, this little ten-year old girl decided to be a journalist.

My motivation for becoming a journalist clearly stemmed from my experiences and witnessing first-hand that broadcasting information to the world can either contribute to creating fear or create a better world. I wanted the latter - to give hope and shine a light, in order to illustrate the good in society. I wanted to share information with the world that was beneficial, inspirational and life-changing.

This moment created magic: The 'aha' moment of deciding to bring inspirational news to the world, coupled with my younger-self's mantra of, 'I can do anything through Christ'. What's the magic? Well, I didn't know it at the time, and I only recently discovered it. The magic of my childhood and teenage years defined my 'Why' for me.

So, this comes back to me asking, 'What's my why?' Well, it's to bring raw, fun and intimate moments to television screens to inspire, entertain and change lives.

So, I ask you to self-reflect.

Delve into your history and look at your story.

Everybody has a story and there is something to be learned from every experience. It's through your experiences that you will uncover your true self – some memories may be painful, some uncomfortable, and some will cause heartache, but it's these experiences that have led you to the chosen path. Success is attributed to past experiences; we learn and grow from the past. To be successful, it's important to acknowledge and uncover your memoir and upbringing.

I believe that the way you were raised and treated in the world, is a reflection of how you treat other people. Your spiritual beliefs and your thought-driven beliefs determine your course of actions. Your beliefs shape what you become. I believe that I can accomplish anything, because I have been given divine power from on high, through the grace of God.

This belief is ingrained in me, and I have entered this world with the understanding that no matter what challenges I face, I can always rely on God for support. Do you have confidence that your belief shapes what you become? The mind is a powerful tool, some even call it a weapon. What thoughts fuel your mind? What ammunition do you feed it? We all pay attention to our bodies, and ensure our physical health is at peak performance. We eat well, exercise, keep hydrated, reduce our alcohol consumption, and quit smoking. We can see our bodies, so it's a constant reminder we need to nurture and nourish ourselves physically.

We look after our bodies to continue living, moving, and performing our daily habits. The mind, however, is a forgotten appendage. Since we can't see it, it is sometimes neglected. What are you doing to nurture and nourish your mind? Your mind is the most valuable asset that can either flourish your life or destroy it.

Looking back, I developed a 'yes' mindset very early on.

This mindset changed my life.

I credit that to my family and extended family. I say 'yes' to any opportunities that present themselves and I embrace change. Couple this 'yes' mentality with my stubborn belief of, 'I believe I can do all things' and I became an unstoppable force in my teenage years. I tapped into that 'success-mindset' that many people speak of from a young age.

Being young, I didn't do anything myself to achieve this type of thinking – how could I? I was young and influenced by my family. I can't take any credit for what I now recognise to be a successful mindset mentality.

I attribute my success-mindset to my dad, who from the young age of eleven years old, taught me to be fearless and bold. Our ethnic community, Egyptian specifically, define success as a career- What you do determines your success. In 1996, I completed my Year 12 HSC and was ready to tackle my life's greatest ambition, to be a TV presenter and journalist.

According to the general Egyptian community, you are only successful if you are a doctor of some sort, a pharmacist, an engineer, or a lawyer.

No other career defines you as successful. In the 1990's, this narrow-minded way of thinking was widely acceptable, and many in our community were therefore labelled as failures in life. I was one of them.

When I proudly announced I was accepted at university to study a Bachelor of Journalism and Media Production, I was met with disappointment and pretentious smiles. Had my dad not prepared me from a young age to be daring and think big, I would have changed my degree to appease the community and regretted it forever.

So, what exactly did my dad do or say when I was 11 years old?

He knew I wanted to be a TV presenter and journalist. He also knew the reaction I would receive from the community in following this career path. His prudent words of affirmation and strength were exactly this, "Suzy, do whatever you want, as long as it meets these three criteria: Number one: Is it illegal? Number two: Would God disapprove? And Number three: Does it harm you or others?

If the answer is yes to any of these, don't do it. If not, go for your life, and don't give a damn what anyone else thinks of you. You're not doing anything shameful or wrong."

Needless to say, my dad is my hero.

He was my first influencer. He is a rarity to have in my corner, and I am blessed to have been raised by an open-minded, loving, intelligent soul that has such courage and valour. I hope you have someone like this in your corner too.

As I grew, my perception of God grew with me. I understood what it meant to be part of creation, and that God controlled the universe. There are forces that people speak of but can't associate them to a higher being. That association with my spirituality and the energy of the universe made sense to me, as I was experiencing it from a Christian belief. My belief was accurately articulated by Oprah in one of her podcasts. She said, "I expanded my view of what it means to be a citizen of the universe. To be a part of the energy field that is omnipotent, omniscient, all-knowing, and all-present in all things, and so my confidence comes from knowing there is something greater than myself that I am a part of and is also a part of me.

I call that God, but I do nothing without that understanding.

How I think one masters one's life is to understand that you are cocreating that life with the ultimate creator. Not understanding that puts you at your own pitiful, meagre, little will, and everything is left up to you, and you can't do it.

You cannot survive in this world by yourself just believing in yourself. You're not big enough to do it. I'm not big enough to do it. Nobody is big enough to do it. You must understand that your very presence here as a human being here on earth came from something greater than you." Preach it sister!

Every successful woman has a few role models she can learn from. My biggest influence and role model is Oprah. I feel a profound connection to her. At a deeper level, I understand her 'why'. I empathise and appreciate why she did *The Oprah Show* and saw the incredible way her passion and humanity changed lives.

It wasn't just because she had the ability to do it, it was because it felt 'home' to her. Oprah's childhood story tells of her mother's unplanned pregnancy. This placed Oprah in a unique position-she understood what it feels like to not be wanted. She also had an unplanned and unwanted pregnancy and felt a disconnection to her own baby.

She understood the disconnection between her mother not wanting her, as she felt the same disconnection to her baby, who died at birth.

Oprah extended her personal experience to make everyone feel wanted and to know that they matter. She found her 'why' and lived it.

Stepping through the looking glass, I am currently producing my show. It's my 'why'. It feeds people's souls. It connects, challenges, entertains, and has a purpose in society. I feel comfortable and at 'home' when I am on-set speaking to my guests, connecting with them and to my audience.

My show is a platform for engaging and entertaining content to be delivered to viewers. It's my 'why', manifested through a personal journey of growth, resilience, and change. I understand what it feels like to be constantly judged and performing to other people's expectations.

My community expected more from me. They expected me to be a lawyer or engineer. I was expected to be the 'perfect child' as I was the priest's granddaughter, I was labelled a 'good girl', I went to private schools, and continued my education at university.

So, the expectation was to study something 'decent' at university…certainly not media. In my teenage years, I needed to stop the habit of comparing myself to others and stop aspiring to other people's beliefs. Even now, my purpose on this earth is to be the best version of me, not a replica of someone else's unique identity.

Theologian Howard said, "Don't ask yourself what the world needs. Ask yourself what makes you come alive and then go do that. Because what the world needs is people who have come alive."

Media has always been my passion, and it's what makes me come alive. In my late teenage years, while I was studying my Bachelor of Journalism and Media Production, I was submerged in multiple voluntary media undertakings.

I was the host of a morning show on community television, I was an entertainment youth reporter, I produced a documentary with SBS television, I was a talk-back host on radio, and the deputy editor of the university's on-campus magazine.

Looking back now, I see my life was a lesson in excellence. When you do well, when you do your best, people notice. To me, I wasn't doing anything different or extraordinary, because I had been doing charitable deeds since I could walk, it was entrenched in my upbringing.

So, these 'charitable' actions in the media became apparent, and one of my university lecturers nominated me for the *Young Australian of the Year Award* in 2000. I was runner-up, which was an incredible honour, and I still pinch myself every time I recall that moment. I play the scene of my runner-up award acceptance from Prime Minister John Howard, standing next to the winner, Ian Thorpe. John Howard shook my hand and said with a big smile, "Congratulations! Australia needs more people like you to give back to the community."

I was just 21 at the time and Mr Howard's comment fuelled me with exhilaration, drive, purpose and responsibility.

Six months later, I married, and two years after that, I had my first child.

I continued working in media in any way I could: Freelance writing, scripting, and editing video documentaries. I became pregnant within three months and had my second child. In fact, I had four children in five years! I was busy raising children and working between 23-28 years old.

These were the golden years, and I was raising children, while working odd jobs in-between. Of course, I made sacrifices, and of course it was hard. I drew on all my energy, my learnings, and my experiences from my teenage years, to push through. I looked to what was ahead, and what could come from my toil and labour. I was determined to keep going, and not relinquish my media career.

I've worked in television as an international executive producer for Australia, and liaised with the USA, the UK and Canada, to produce shows and features for a global audience. I've been a television presenter, a news anchor, a talk-show host, a deputy editor for four national magazine titles, the editor-in-chief and senior journalist for a local newspaper as well as a television presenter for a streaming channel. I've had a breadth of experience encapsulating all aspects of media, from writing and editing, to presenting and producing. Some people look at the opportunities I've had and call it luck. It's much bigger than luck.

There is a powerful force at work in my life, one that is not based on luck, but rather on a greater plan.

Every aspect of my life has come together in a deliberate and meaningful way. I have been blessed with grace and divine order, and I do not attribute any of it to mere luck. Luck, in my opinion, is reserved for chance events, such as winning the lottery.

My life, on the other hand, has been shaped by planning opportunities. I have been meticulously prepared for every moment of opportunity that has come my way, thanks to the guiding force that directs my hand. Every experience in my life has served a purpose, preparing me for the challenges and prospects that lie ahead.

Along my media travels, I've forfeited a lot. I've failed, I've lost, I've learned, and I've grown. I discovered that the course of my life is determined by the energy behind my intentions. I recognised thisj in my childhood years. While many solely focus on their actions, they neglect to consider the driving force behind them.

However, the energy that you put into your pursuits will ultimately be reflected to you.

You get out what you put in.

Therefore, the true 'why' behind your actions is what truly matters. Regardless of the obstacles you may face, genuine success and happiness are attainable through a singular objective - to embody the most authentic and elevated version of yourself. At times, you will need to be vulnerable to unlock your hidden abilities and full capacity. By striving to maximise your potential and uplift not only yourself, but also those around you, you can fulfil your humanity and find true fulfilment.

Each person's life has a pattern and purpose, and that's how we determine our 'why'. How do you know what your purpose is? How can you recognise it? Quite simply, it feels like your safe space. It feels comfortable. It feels 'right'. The most iconic names in history have found their purpose, and that's why they are iconic. They are influencers and role models.

Take a moment to reflect on your role models, your influencers and your heroes. Why are they special to you? What connects you to them? I've discovered that defining my influencers, unmasks my authentic self.

Desiring to live as my authentic self and not conform to the expectations of others, is a natural inclination for humans – to be themselves. I too, want to be free to live my life on my own terms - to live my best, authentic version of myself.

The human experience shares a common goal - to live authentically and reach our highest potential. This pursuit continues throughout our lives. Regardless of our current circumstances, there's always room for growth towards becoming the best version of ourselves.

Until the moment that I've fully utilised my unique value as an individual, my work is incomplete.
I'm still running the race.
I'm not there to beat anyone, I'm in the race to win for myself – to achieve my goals, my purpose and to continue my contribution to humanity. Every race need training, and I need to train myself to remain

focused on living my best authentic self. The moment I shift my focus to others in the race, the sight of my own journey will be lost. At times, I may face obstacles and challenges along the way, but each one serves as a valuable lesson that provides the necessary growth to reach my unique destination. This is my journey and my purpose. This path is distinct from that of those around me.

Embracing the bumps in the road is key to arriving at my intended direction: My purpose. I'm still travelling and navigating around those bumps. *I believe that the success of life is to progress, and change is an unavoidable part of that process.*

"No one can make you feel inferior without your consent."

— Eleanor Roosevelt

THE SKY IS NOT THE LIMIT, THERE ARE NO LIMITS

SHELLI BRUNSWICK

I am delighted to share with you the exciting journey of my career and my experiences in the global space ecosystem. As the chief operating officer of Space Foundation, I have been fortunate to witness the incredible contributions of diverse individuals in various fields, all working toward space innovation and the betterment of life on Earth. This chapter will explore the opportunities that exist in the space industry, especially for women, and the importance of mentorship in paving the way for a brighter future. I invite you to join me in this thrilling adventure into the world of space and beyond.

Introduction

As COO of Space Foundation, one of the world's leading space advocacy organizations, my journey into space began in the U.S. Air Force, where I served as an Acquisition and Program Management leader before becoming a Congressional liaison. My career has been diverse and expansive, fueled by my passion for championing women in business and increasing their representation in the space industry. Today, I oversee three divisions that contribute to space innovation and drive positive change on our planet: Symposium 365, the Center for Innovation and Education, and Global Alliance.

Space4Women Mentorship Program

One of the most exciting roles and initiatives I am involved in is serving as a mentor for the United Nations' Space4Women mentorship program. This program aims to create sustainable development goals for gender equality and equal education, providing women and girls with access to the space ecosystem. Sharing knowledge and empowering future generations are essential steps in ensuring a future that matters. I am also a mentor for multiple entrepreneurs through the WomenTech Network, which promotes diversity and inclusion in various industries.

The Power of Mentoring

Finding the right mentor who aligns with your beliefs and values can be transformative for your career. A mentor-mentee relationship can help overcome challenges and pave the way for success. It is a mutual relationship, as mentors also learn from their mentees. Regardless of your stage of life or career, a mentoring relationship can fuel personal and professional growth.

Space: Beyond Astronauts and Satellites

When most people think of a career in space, they often envision astronauts and satellites. However, the space industry is vast and diverse, offering opportunities for professionals from various backgrounds — not just STEM or IT experts. Journalists, HR professionals, policy makers, educators and others all contribute to the space ecosystem in meaningful ways. The space industry has become commercialised, making it accessible to anyone with passion and determination.

Space Technology in Diverse Sectors

The space industry intersects with numerous sectors, including agriculture, healthcare, education, transportation, communication, public relations, finance and cybersecurity. Space technology, such as precision agriculture, can improve crop yields and sustainability. It can also aid in determining water usage and provide opportunities for growing food and resources on other planets. The reciprocal learning between space and Earth has resulted in groundbreaking innovations across multiple industries.

Inclusion and Diversity in the Space Industry

The space industry has evolved to become more inclusive and diverse. While gender inequality was once a prevalent issue, organizations like Space Foundation and programs like Space4Women have driven positive change. By highlighting the accomplishments of women and minorities in the space industry, we can inspire future generations to pursue their dreams without constraints.

The Promising Future of the Space Industry

The global space ecosystem is thriving, and the industry is expected to grow significantly in the coming years. With thousands of pending patents waiting for innovative application and commercialization, the space economy is projected to be worth trillions of dollars in the near future. As we explore the possibilities of settlements and research centers as well as our existence on other planets, the space industry needs new talents with a diversity of backgrounds, ages and ethnicities from various regions of the world to contribute their skills and expertise.

Conclusion

The global space ecosystem offers boundless opportunities for individuals from all walks of life. Together, we can inspire future generations and create a world that embraces diversity, equality and inclusion. As we continue to explore the mysteries of space, let us also remember our responsibility to care for our planet and ensure a sustainable future. Join me on this journey to foster a thriving and inclusive space industry, where every dreamer can find their place among the stars. Together, we can do great things!

Acknowledgments

I would like to express my deepest gratitude to all the mentors, mentees and colleagues who have supported and inspired me throughout my career. Your guidance and encouragement have been invaluable in shaping my passion for space and promoting diversity in the industry. Thank you for believing in the limitless potential of humanity and for working tirelessly to make the world a better place.

"I've come to believe that each of us has a personal calling that's as unique as a fingerprint – and that the best way to succeed is to discover what you love and then find a way to offer it to others in the form of service, working hard, and also allowing the energy of the universe to lead you."

— *Oprah Winfrey*

MY LIFE IS A PERFECT JIGSAW

PATRICIA GROVER

My name is Patricia Jo Grover, and I am known as 'The Goal Achievement Strategist.' In this memoir, I will share my journey of overcoming challenges and achieving success, in both my personal and professional life.

I came from a childhood that most people couldn't conceive, let alone believe. I never saw what a happy home life was supposed to be, or what a healthy relationship, between a man and a woman, was supposed to look like.

My life was a product of domestic abuse, due to my father having been an alcoholic. My mother, after barely surviving his reign, tried her best to provide for me the best that she could, which led her to having our home become one of the first adult foster homes, for patients from the mental hospital that she worked at as a nurse. It was in a bedroom, just two doors down from mine, where I found my first dead body at age seven, with the next by age 12. Kids didn't come over to my house to play, and I always tried to stay out of the house as much as possible.

Because of not really having what anyone would actually consider a childhood, as well as being exposed to so much that was way beyond what most children had ever had to see or deal with, I matured before my time. When I was away from home, I was making bad choices of who I was spending time with, and what I was spending time doing. I was putting myself into situations that were unhealthy for me in many ways.

Although I eventually ran away from home, I was from a small town and didn't have any money, so didn't make it very far. Through babysitting, I saved enough money to buy my first car when I was 15, because I wanted to be able to get away.

When I did, I got in way over my head hanging out with the wrong people and doing wrong things. By the time that I was 16, I had gotten out into the world and experienced things that of course I wish I hadn't but had to accept that I had only done it to myself because of the choices that I had made.

I realised I was on the wrong path and knew that I wanted more out of life than what I had already experienced myself or seen in the lives of the people that I had been exposed to. My mother always said, 'you are who you hang out with'. She also said, when she found herself not doing too much of anything and relaxing a bit that, 'this isn't going to buy the baby any new shoes.

I was determined to find a way to create a path for myself. I chose to start taking my education more seriously and found something that I was passionate about, something I decided I wanted to try to make a career out of. I also got a job waiting tables, so that I would be able to start living in my own place, as soon as possible.

My career choice was Cosmetology and I ended up going to High School and Beauty School at the same time, while I was in my Senior Year. Graduating both schools, within months of each other, I then went out and got my first job in the industry.

Now being 18 and thinking that I had the world by the seat of the pants, I thought I was ready to get into a serious relationship. I wanted attention and affection from someone who I now trusted, not to mirror the things I had experienced when I was younger, with people that I should never have been around to begin with. At this point, being 18 and feeling like I knew I had it made, having experienced more adult things, I tended to be a little more on the wild side and liked to do my share of partying and drinking.

My first serious boyfriend, the brother of my best friend, also became my first husband. It lasted about a year, with him getting two OUI's in two days, and being a black-out drunk.

Note, I said 'first' boyfriend.

After him, came my daughter's father, whom I ended up leaving when I was three months pregnant, when I realised that he was not going to be there for me, or my child. I was 20 years old when she was born.

Then came husband number two, who was an only child from a military family and who had been used to moving around but was also what is known as a military brat. He had always been spoiled, getting everything, he wanted, and never had to be responsible for anything.

We ended up getting into over $20,000 in credit card debt, and when we got divorced, we were both ordered to pay half. Which I did, but he didn't, and because my name was also on the cards, I ended up having to declare bankruptcy.

My brother had come home from being in the Navy, during the time I was with my second husband. After leaving, he ended up in San Diego, where he became a male prostitute and drug dealer, to make money to cover the cost of the drugs that he was using.

When my brother finally returned home at age 30, he came out to our family that he had been living his life as a gay man for quite some time, but because of his IV drug use, he was now also HIV Positive.

My brother was the closest in age to me, nine years older than me. He and I had experienced what life was like with our father and then living in my mother's first boarding home. He was the closest relationship that I had ever had at that point in my life, so of course I was going to love and support him in any way that I could through his battle with his health.

At that time, there wasn't a lot known about HIV or AIDS and as a result, society was not as receptive to having people that had been diagnosed participating in everyday activities around them.
My brother became the President of our Local AIDS Network and attended schools and hospitals, as well as different events to raise awareness and educate people to make as big of a difference for future generations as possible.

I supported him in all that he did.

Knowing my brother my entire life at that point, I can tell anyone without a doubt, that homosexuality is not a choice. His alcoholism began at an early age, as he tried to hide from what he was, that then turned to drug use, which just completely spun out of control.

Seeing as though he was my brother and given the fact I loved him, I chose to raise my daughter around him, being the best family that we could all be for one another, until he died five years later. I faced ridicule from people for doing so, but knew that we were not putting her, or myself, in any danger of being infected. In my view, family had to come first.

To this point, I was still in the beauty industry and had worked at a few different salons. I was also doing education for companies, such as Matrix Essentials, KMS and Jessica Cosmetics, about their skincare, cosmetics, hair colours, perms and so on.

I became a registered Massage Practitioner and was working with wigs for cancer patients at the hospital. I was the Assistant Manager at the salon where I was working, when I actually met my third husband, a client of mine.

He had been getting his haircuts from me the whole time I was going through everything with my brother and the divorce from my second husband.

After my divorce from my second husband was final and my brother had passed away, I didn't jump into any other marriages right away, but did end up in a couple of relationships. One was short lived, and the other was an engagement to a man who had the sweetest, kindest, most loving heart.

But that didn't last long either, because I realised that since my daughter at that time was in fourth grade, she could read better than he could. And although he was wonderful with both of us, he was not going to be able to be the husband and father that I wanted for myself and my daughter, let alone the father to any additional children we might have.

After that relationship ended, I got together with my third husband. The one I mentioned had been one of my clients. Following the death of my brother and my second divorce, I decided to venture out into the salon business on my own. I opened a Salon & Day Spa, with six female staff and a tanning bed. I even brought in my own private label line of Skincare and Cosmetics.

So, I was dealing with the challenges of raising a child as a single parent, running a business, and trying to have relationships, all at the same time.

During that time, friends and clients used to tell me, when I mentioned how tired I was, "That's funny, you make everything that you do look so easy. All of your staff, and even your daughter, have no idea what it takes from you to pull all of this off."

Then I got into the relationship with my third husband who had seen what I had been through and saw where I was at now. By this time, my daughter was nine, and with us moving to his home, away from her friends, it didn't go over so well. You see, he was a man who I found out also thought that I made things look so easy. Because it wasn't what had to happen, to make everything look perfect to him that mattered.

He actually wanted everything, including me, the house, cars, and my daughter, to be perfect all the time. And she was resentful for having to move away from friends and unhappy with his expectations and would say, "You aren't my real father, you can't tell me what to do". He had a son, from a previous relationship, who was already a teenager and so he had actually never parented. He really didn't like what comes along with parenting, and finally admitted that he really only wanted me.

That was only after endless battles between him and my daughter, who would say and do things to piss him off intentionally, and with him thinking that being extra hard on her would break her. It was a horrible experience for all involved.

So, I have shared all about my failed relationships to point out the fact I never saw what a healthy happy relationship between a man and a woman was supposed to look like, or how to actually have one.

I was just out there looking for something, but I just didn't know what. For the record, all of these men were completely different; it wasn't like I kept going back to the same type of guy.

After that third divorce, I was so down on myself, asking what was so wrong with me that I couldn't seem to find happiness. What puzzle pieces was I missing?

So, I chose to dig deep within myself and dismantle the puzzle pieces that had made me who I had become to that point. As I started putting those pieces back together again, one by one, I grew to Know, Like, Trust and ultimately, Love myself.

It was then, I developed my philosophy that life is like a 'Jigsaw Puzzle', and that I started to rough together the tools and therapies that I use today as part of my proprietary, 'Conquering Skills Education'.

You see, at that time of my life I was in my late twenties and all the motivational speakers and authors who wrote about personal growth were older men. So, I spent thousands of hours reading self-help books, attending conferences, listening to speakers, and finding mentors. But despite all of these efforts, I still wasn't successful in finding what I really needed.

By this time, I had to take on additional work and had begun a career in management within the Health and Beauty industry, in order to be able to have health insurance for myself and my daughter. As I delved deeper into research, I discovered the secret to absorbing knowledge from other people's wisdom.

I learned that success is not only about what you know, but also about how you apply that knowledge. So, I worked with what I had been able to learn and created the first drafts of what I needed. I then began to apply my new-found knowledge and started to see results. With time, I achieved success in my personal and professional life, and knew I had found my calling.

If what I had created had worked for me, I knew that it would be able to help others as well.

But the timing wasn't right, nine years had passed as I was retaking, reshaping, and remaking my life. Now that I felt whole, and no longer looking for pieces of myself in another person, I found husband number four.

When we met, I was a District Sales Manager for Avon Products Inc. managing over 400 Avon ladies in my State. I had a company car and was travelling 1000 miles per week, teaching them about the products, how to operate a profitable business, as well as how to host skin and cosmetic parties.

I had to kiss a lot of toads before I found this prince.

We were inseparable after our third date, when he asked me to marry him. We lived our lives with adventure and passion, enjoying each other and the world around us. We had similar interests, and the world was our oyster.

It wasn't too long after we were married that we decided that we wanted to become snowbirds and move to Florida. I gave up my job with Avon and we were about to start a business that was based in Florida but could operate anywhere.

Unfortunately, we ended up having a bad motorcycle accident on December 4, 2010, that I'm lucky to be alive after. I suffered a TBI, fractured skull and a brain bleed. I blew out my right eardrum and had a torn rotator cuff. I don't remember the accident, the ambulance, being airlifted, or my week in intensive care. I don't remember about a month of my life. I couldn't smell or taste things for a long time. I would have panic attacks just being a passenger in a car. I never thought that I'd be able to drive again.

After healing, we decided that life was too short, so we wanted to do something that had been on both of our bucket lists. We became franchisees of a KOA Kampground. We owned and operated it for seven years, while we were still able to be snowbirds. We doubled the business and were able to sell it for a profit. Throughout this entire time, we'd also been living in our 40 ft motorhome.

When we sold the Campground in August of 2017, I decided to start writing my first book from all of the notes that I had made so many years ago, and with all of the knowledge and experience that I had gained since.

The week after I started writing the book, my husband was diagnosed with Mantle Cell Lymphoma, which is non curable and reoccurring.

He was given two to five years to live. We weren't going to take this lying down, so we got him into a clinical trial at MD Anderson in Houston Texas, with the best doctor in the country.

We moved our motorhome to live in Houston, and while he was in the hospital and undergoing treatments, I launched my first book.

However, shortly afterwards, the hybrid publishing company that I had used closed their doors and went out of business. They were the ones that had opened my Amazon, Barnes and Noble, and Books-A-Million accounts. So, I ended up having to get a new ISBN and doing a complete rewrite.

Since we no longer needed to be in Houston full- time, we sold the motorhome and purchased a home in Maine, where on our 25 acres of land, we put an 18-hole Disc Golf Course.

With the Second Edition of my book becoming an International Best Seller in the U.S. and Canada, I decided to create my platform.

I wanted to help others achieve the same level of success that I had, and that's how I became a goal achievement strategist, speaker, coach, mentor and host. I created my platform to encourage, educate, and empower individuals to achieve more success in their lives and be able to 'Rise Above' any challenges they may have in any of the eight dimensions of life. These dimensions include physical, emotional, intellectual, spiritual, social, environmental, occupational and financial.

I believe that success is subjective and varies from person to person, and I encourage individuals to connect their purpose and their 'why' with their sensory vision. By doing so, individuals can become emotionally connected with their dream, making them unstoppable in achieving their goals.

In my book, "Living Outside the Box," I provide a personal GPS system for goal achievement that empowers readers to break the cycles of limiting beliefs, while they are solving the jigsaw puzzles that are their lives. The book offers not only suggestions and advice, but also proven exercises and activities designed to facilitate the process of liberating individuals so they can achieve their goals.

With my "Rise Above" platform I have the Show, Podcast, Academy, and B.L.I.S.S. Events that I utilise my proprietary "Conquering Skills Education". All things "Rise Above" with Patricia

Jo Grover, ties to the fact that I am a philanthropist who has her own non-profit, "The Rise Above Project," under the umbrella of "The Institute for the Advancement of Humanity" (a 501c3) organisation. The project's mission is to improve the lives of women and children, who have been victims of domestic abuse and to aid those who may be disadvantaged and may not have learned both life and soft skills but are ready to "Rise Above" their challenges.

I am proud of the work that I have done, and I am grateful for the opportunity to help others achieve their dreams. I believe that everyone has the potential to have more, do more, and be more if that is what they want. However, I acknowledge that not everyone may desire to achieve more, and that is perfectly okay.

As I reflect on my journey, I am reminded of the puzzle pieces that make up our lives. Each piece represents a different phase or experience, and it is up to us to put the pieces together to create the picture that we want. I have spent my life helping individuals put the pieces together, and I am proud of the work I have done.

As a goal achievement strategist, my work is focused on empowering individuals to take control of their lives and achieving success in all areas. I believe that success is not just about achieving your goals, but also about the journey and the personal growth that comes along the way.

One of the core principles of my work is the idea that success is subjective and varies from person to person. I encourage individuals to connect with their purpose and their why, to identify what success means to them and to create a clear vision of what they want to achieve.

Through my coaching and mentoring work, I have seen firsthand, the transformative power of setting clear goals and taking consistent action towards them. Many of my clients have been able to achieve success in their personal and professional lives, overcome obstacles and challenges, and create fulfilling and purposeful lives.

My book, "Living Outside the Box," is a personal GPS system to goal achievement that offers readers practical strategies and tools to help them break free from limiting beliefs and achieve their goals. It is designed to guide readers through a process of self-discovery and growth, helping them to identify their strengths, values, and purpose, and to create a clear roadmap to success.

In the book, I share my own personal journey of growth and self-discovery, including the challenges and obstacles I have faced along the way. I believe that by sharing our stories and experiences, we can inspire others and help them to see that they are not alone in their struggles.

I am also a firm believer in the power of community and connection.

Through my work, I have seen how connecting with others, who share similar goals and values, can be a powerful catalyst for growth and transformation. That is why I have created a community of like-minded individuals, who are committed to achieving their goals and supporting each other along the way.

One of the things that sets my approach apart is the emphasis on the eight dimensions of life. I believe that true success and fulfilment come from achieving balance and growth in all areas of life, including physical, emotional, intellectual, spiritual, social, environmental, occupational, and financial.

By focusing on these eight dimensions and creating goals in each area, individuals can create a holistic and fulfilling life that aligns with their values and purpose. It's not just about achieving success in one area of life, but about creating a life that is balanced and meaningful.

I am also passionate about giving back and making a positive impact on the world. That is why I have founded a non-profit organisation, "The Rise Above Project," which is dedicated to improving the lives of women and children who have been victims of domestic abuse, and to helping those who may be disadvantaged and in need of support.

Through "The Rise Above Project," we provide education, resources, and support to help individuals overcome their challenges and achieve their goals. We also work to raise awareness about the issue of domestic abuse and to advocate for change at the community and policy level.

My husband was taken from me four years and 5 months after being given 2 -5 years to live. We had chosen to live what time we had together to its' fullest. Sadly, it wasn't even MCL that he died from, it was the Powassan Virus that stole him from me. The last kiss I gave him, both of us had to wear masks due to Covid Protocol.

Following this, he became paralysed, lost his eyesight, and went into a coma in just four days. Spending a week and a half in our local hospital having them not being able to figure out what was wrong with him, then having to life flight him to Boston to go to Mass General, where Harvard Trained Medical Doctors couldn't figure out what was wrong with him, after another week and a half either.

I had to make the decision to pull the plug. Then had them do an autopsy. It wasn't until after he was cremated that those results came back saying it was Encephalitis. Then, after the test results finally came back to Mass General saying it was the Powassan Virus, they had to contact the National Center for Disease Control, who then had to do a National Press Release.

I had to take off almost an entire year to heal, and in that time created other therapies that I now use in my platform.

As once again I had found myself in the need to Retaking, Reshaping, and Remaking both my personal and professional life. I walk my own talk daily as I continue to live my life to my own fullest potential. And I choose to do it Purposefully, Joyfully, and Gratefully.

I've now written a Growth and Gratitude Journal, and as a companion to "Living Outside the Box", the "Design Your Destiny

Planning System". I've submitted chapters to several Anthology Book Series and spoken at many events for women all over the globe.

Overall, my journey has taught me that anything is possible if you have a clear vision, a strong sense of purpose, and the willingness to take consistent action towards your goals.

I am grateful for the opportunities that have come my way, and I am committed to continuing to empower individuals to achieve success and create fulfilling lives. I myself have become a Master of Retaking, Reshaping, and Remaking my own life, so that I can Have, Be, Do, and Earn more, while living my life Purposefully, Joyfully and Gratefully.

As I reflect on my journey, I am reminded of the quote by Ralph Waldo Emerson, "Life is a journey, not a destination." For me, success is not just about achieving a specific goal or outcome, but about the growth and transformation along the way. It is about embracing the journey and being present in each moment, knowing that every experience is an opportunity for learning and growth.

In conclusion, my life's work as a goal achievement strategist, speaker and author, has been centred around empowering individuals to achieve their dreams, and create fulfilling lives.

"My will shall shape the future. Whether I fail or succeed shall be no one's doing but my own. I am the force. I can clear any obstacle before me or I can be lost in the maze. My choice. My responsibility. Win or lose; only I hold the key to my destiny."

— Elaine Maxwell

SETTING EXTRODINARY GOALS

LAYNE BEACHLEY

At just eight years old, my dad told me I was adopted and in turn, this became the catalyst to my success. I felt that I needed to prove I was worthy, and loveable and becoming a world champion surfer was my way to do that. When I joined the professional surfing tour in 1990, the history books noted that the record for the number of championships won for a woman was four, and for a man, five. In my determination, I knew that my goal was to hit the big, golden number six. In a row.

Through blood, sweat, tears, pain, and suffering, I reached my goal, and became the first woman and only surfer to win six consecutive world championships. After the initial euphoria and elation, fatigue and exhaustion set in.

Looking back now, my first five titles required a great deal of effort, but the sixth felt like a burden. Although I was on top of my game, my body was falling apart. Living life on constant adrenaline can make a person feel limitless, but sooner or later, the body needs a break. It was my physical self that forced me, or offered, me permission to rest, recuperate and pause.

Sometimes, we don't offer ourselves the slack we deserve, but the greatest gift we can give ourselves, regardless of our occupation, is stillness. Which for an athlete can feel incredibly counter-intuitive but knowing your 'edge' is everything.

Most of us have felt the brink of exhaustion, and ignoring the signs, big or small, is 'mission critical'.

So, that is what I did, I stopped.

However, my inner competitor was itching to hit the waves again, and so I set myself a new goal: To win my seventh surfing world championship title. This was error number one. I ignored my body, which was screaming at me to lessen the hours of intense training; Over the years I had suffered a rotated pelvis, fractured coccyx, multiple knee injuries, a broken nose and a fractured rib. I was also harbouring a serious neck injury.

At this point, my body was screaming, "Layne, are you listening? I need you to stop. Please stop!"

Between winning my sixth consecutive world title and training for my seventh, there were times when my body was really just going through the motions, without the nurturing and support that it needed. So, once again, I was noticing the effects of adrenal fatigue. I was unable to maintain a sense of concentration and the red flags were bigger than ever.

I nourished my body with a healthy and nutritious diet, and physically, I was training harder than ever.

This is such a common ethos of athletes and ironically, even though the body is the vehicle to success, it's also the one element that can make or break a career in sports.

All of us are masters at fooling ourselves if our instincts don't always align with our plans. Whilst I had my eye on the prize of a seventh title, I knew I was suffering internally. I had zero compassion for myself, physically, emotionally, or mentally.

For years, I knew that I was not only proving myself as a professional surfer, but I was also proving to my eight-year-old self that I wasn't faulty, broken, or rejected. I was craving love and validation in the absence of being able to offer that to myself. Externally and extremely, I was pushing myself harder and harder, attempting to fill the void that remained, since discovering my mother had given me up for adoption at birth.

As a child, this knowledge was so hard to process, and let me tell you, as an adult, it's not that much easier.

Then, realisation of what I was doing and how I was hit. It felt like an awakening when I finally asked myself, "What am I trying to prove? And to who?

Who is Layne Beachley if she isn't winning on the waves?

It was quite an awakening. However, me being me, I needed that seventh title. I was battling with one half of me that was in desperate need of rest, and also with the voice in my head saying, "You can do it. Just one last go".

Whilst on tour in Tahiti, an almighty wave landed on my neck. My left arm went immediately numb, and it stayed like that for five more years. But I ignored it. I continued to persevere to the point where I would surf with a foam pad in my wetsuit to hold my head up because I had lost all strength in my neck and arm.

Really, as I write this, I cannot believe how insane my behaviour was. It was reckless, senseless, and out of control.

During one particular photo shoot, I put my board down and I felt something snap between my shoulder blades. I was rushed off to get an MRI that indicated my disc had herniated so severely it was severing 80 percent of my spinal cord. My doctor gave me two pieces of advice, either retire or get surgery. Neither appealed to me, so I went searching for a second opinion.

Here's the thing about being a self-confessed control freak, when I am surfing, I feel free. My body is required to adapt at a moment's notice, to trust in mother nature. Yet on land, I need to be in control of everything. The ocean brings me peace, dry land does not.

However, I was living in serious risk and finally, I was willing to truly surrender.

For six long months, I did everything and anything to recover in all aspects of my life. Yoga, meditation, hyperbaric chamber, traction therapy, acupuncture, nutritionists, biosync, therapy and more. Some would say my life looked like a permanent retreat, but internally, my mind and body were screaming. I would sit on the water's edge as though the ocean had just broken up with me. It was painful, lonely, and incredibly challenging.

But I did it. I had to choose life, even if it meant turning my back on surfing, to offer love back to myself.

And I did.

I won that seventh title a year after my six-month intensive self-care regime.

Looking back, I now understand that titles two to six were won because I needed to feel love. However, titles number one and seven was because I felt love, my love.

In 2015, I was appointed an Officer of the Order of Australia, a title and acknowledgement that I am so immensely proud and grateful for. It was one of those 'pinch me moments' that has altered my life in so many ways.

Ever since I was a timid and sad eight-year-old girl, I never believed or felt my worth. My self-esteem was measured, or so I once believed, on how many trophies I could lift into the air. My self-compassion was almost redundant, as I waited for the crowds to applaud me, reminding me that I have a place on this planet. Now, I don't go in search of my worth because I feel it, trophy, or no trophy.

As an avid entrepreneur, director, and environmentalist, I have got so much to offer, and despite the injuries and setbacks, they were entirely meant for me.

Without these hurdles and challenges, I would never have been given the gift of patience and insight. It was during these dark and bleak periods in my life, without my surfboard in tow, I saw what I was truly capable of achieving.

As a businesswoman and retired athlete, I now see it as my duty to ensure the formulas for success are shared far and wide. Throughout my career as a speaker and motivational mentor to so many young women, and girls, I am beginning to think we overcomplicate true success. In ways, we over complicate self-awareness and emotional intelligence. Women feel the need to justify their success and defend their choices.

Why can't it be what it needs to be? Why do we struggle with the word 'no' when it comes to business decisions and value alignment?

We need to embrace our truth and remain true to who we are. We don't need to apologise for our ideas or go with the flock. Our individualism needs to be celebrated and plucked from the crowds. Simply uniqueness is everything.

Once you've learnt this incredible truth, which despite sounding really simple, is true. Through my mentoring and coaching business, this is one of the biggest key issues that women, in particular, find very challenging. The amount of people who say, "How do I know what my purpose is?" truly surprises me.

I always reply, "The answers are within you. Trust them. Trust you. It's what you love. It's what makes you smile. It's what makes you breathe. It's what motivates you. It actually is in *you*. It just has to be found."

A friend who worked for a leading Australian bank, suggested that I create my own foundation. I was insanely excited at the prospect of giving back to society and launched 'Aim For the Stars' foundation. The foundation was built on the concept of women empowering one another.

I believe that when we can provide our future women with hope, there is no better use of our own success. Since moving on from the foundation, I look back now and reflect on how each and every one of us need to feel a sense of belonging. After all, my entire career was built off feeling the need to be accepted.

Now, I am all about awakening self-love, which inspired me to launch 'Awake Academy'.

This is a centre for self-empowerment, cultivating connection, growth, and happiness in humanity. We started Awake Academy with the desire to awaken people to detach from fear, take control and design a life they love. Understanding unwanted feelings is the first step to overcoming them. The learnings come from my own personal journey of awakening. Unlike most other courses that are based on studies and generalisations, we aim to provide very real and easy-to-digest truths, in a relevant and engaging format.

Everybody can achieve incredible things in this world, but it requires practical guidance, mentoring and belief. There are so many stories we tell ourselves that prevent us from evolving and transforming hardship into a happy outcome. Even now, I have to turn down the volume on inner chatter that will hinder over helping me. We must always flip the negative, if we are not acting or behaving from a place of love.

> "*A lot of people are afraid to say what they want. That's why they don't get what they want.*"
>
> — *Madonna*

PROSPEROUS PRIESTESS: MY JOURNEY FROM SHADOW AND SCARCITY TO SERVICE, SELF-CARE, AND SACRED SUCCESS

REV. JOSLYN FARRAY PIERRE

Have you ever seen a peacock trying to be an ibis, or an eagle pretending to be a chicken? Surely, that would be a struggle. Well, for an extremely long time, I lived my life and operated my business as a Spiritual and Wellbeing entrepreneur, in the shadows of success. I lived a life playing hide and seek with myself, and constantly fell prey to the illusion of lack and scarcity, buying into fearful thoughts and words.

I felt like a little child on a beautiful exotic Caribbean Island, filled with rich luscious greeneries and bright, luxurious multi-coloured foliage, walking down a magnificent trail, with a mixture of spicy and delicious aromas blowing on the wings of a gentle cool breeze, leading to the end of this vast oasis, with a gentle ocean ushering me to come and play in the cooling water.

I often felt I was constantly standing at the edge, dipping my toes in, testing the waters, liking how it felt, sometimes even putting both feet in, and walking into the waters, beginning to swim.

Sometimes, I even launched into the deep, but as soon as I was approached by any creature, big or small, I returned with haste to the periphery, gazing longingly at what could have been mine, but also encouraging and cheerleading others to experience it for themselves.

This was me longing, but feeling unqualified, unworthy, and not enough to fully engage in business, because of the circumstances and situations I was faced with. Despite enduring significant challenges, I always tried to overcome them with all the finesse and gusto in the world.

All my life I wanted to own a business in health, wellness, and wellbeing.

I remember that even as a teenager, I wanted to be a nutritionist and operate my own health food store. Later as my knowledge and experience expanded, that idea evolved into wanting my own fitness and nutrition club and gym.

This idea gave birth, first starting a small club hosting free aerobics and nutrition classes in my neighbour's downstairs apartment, to later moving to another relative's house, followed by a huge shift to renting a house for my home- based business, a holistic fitness and nutrition club.

Back then, holistic health in my country was not a big deal and was barely considered, let alone known about. My plans were to cater to an individual's body, mind, and spirit, using my spiritual knowledge and experience of my personal experiences and training. I also put to use my professional training as a food, nutrition, health and wellness expert, as well the support I received from my loving spouse.

Together, we worked on this new business venture, whilst also holding down jobs as educators, growing our family and tending to ministry work within our local church. I was excited and willing to go all out to get the business up and running.

However, at that stage, I didn't know I was in for a rude awakening and a long walk into learning about business. Thus, my journey in regards to cultivating a purposeful business began, and I learned to recognise how much I was romanticising the whole idea. I realised I was in love with how my business appeared, rather than loving the business enough to let it breathe and have a life of its own.

In retrospect, this was the time, as my late great grandmother would say, 'I didn't want to crawl, before I walked'. I skipped steps and reached for shiny objects, or ran to start big, rather than small. By now, you can guess, this didn't end well and unfortunately this business venture, despite heavily investing in it financially, emotionally, and otherwise, did not get off the ground.

Not only did I lose my finances with the business, as well as a potential investment in a larger home, but my marriage also came under major stress. I felt more vulnerable than ever and ended up compromising my personal values to compensate for the loss.

The lessons continued and me and another colleague decided we would apply for a business loan to carry out another massive business operation, opening a state-of-the-art gym in our country. We went all out regarding our dreaming, visioning, planning and proposals.

Again, I was in love with the glitz and glamour of business, wanting to be seen as a huge success, without the process of actually doing the work. As a budding entrepreneur, these sorts of manifestations led to many still- births and miscarriages in business. This particular new gym venture was a miscarriage and once again, did not come to full term.

The bank didn't approve our loan and my business partner left, without a word, to open another type of business on their own. My great grandma would say I had to 'put my tail between my legs as a cut tail dog, lick my wounds and carry on.'

Life had to continue, and I carried on as best as I knew how.

Building the foundation for my business, as I now know it, has been one of sheer grits, with a rare trust in goodness and God. The bricks laid in the formative years of this business, were made from a series of painful upheavals in my once loving, stable and model relationship, aka my marriage. From having to move from living as a nuclear family unit, to an extended family unit, to having to figure out the roles and assert myself as wife, mother, friend, career woman, entrepreneur and relative, was a puzzle.

Being a born crowd pleaser and obsessed with aesthetics, was neither a comfortable or profitable job. Added to this came the loss of close family members, starting with my great grandmother, followed by my father-in-law. Then came the most heart-wrenching, never anticipated day that no parent wants to hear about or live through. A beautiful, enchanting day, filled with youthful vibrant vigour, laughter, joy, the smell of the fresh breeze mingling with a clean aroma of freshly cut grass.

A little boy skipping happily as he savoured all that life could offer in a day. From preparing for Christmas shopping, to getting a sample view of the many toys he could choose from, to gleefully welcoming grandpa and chatting with his 'papa' as he affectionately called him, as he accompanied him with landscaping duties of our home.

The day continued and we began making preparations to leave for spiritual duties at our local church. Our little Prince Kwame, bubbling with energy, was outside with papa, while we got ready to leave, preparing the car seat, baby formula and so on for our little five-month-old beauty and princess, Jemima.

Given that Prince Kwame seemed to be pretty busy and taking much joy in being with his grandfather, his father and I decided we'd leave without him. However, at the last minute, Kwame gently got into the car, opting to be with his little sister.

It was from there the amazing and beautiful day turned into a nightmare; one you wish was only a dream.

That trip, which was supposed to be a few hours of separation from our kids, turned out to be a permanent separation from our precious little boy, leaving us to mourn and grieve his death, while gathering the courage to continue to live for our little princess Jemima.

It didn't stop there, while still putting the pieces together and recovering, Kwame's Health and Fitness Club (KHFC) was launched. It was going well, until I decided it was time to go big, and launched out into the deep. And deep it was.

Before I knew it, I was overwhelmed and I felt I didn't have the finances, or support from my spouse. The project failed and we had to relocate. It was during this tumultuous time, still recovering from the loss of our baby boy, the business failure, and other personal failures right on our heels, that on the anniversary of our son's passing, my brother in-law, whom we had a close relationship with and who lived in the same house as us, went to bed and died unexpectedly.

One night he was playing piano with our daughter, and the next morning we found him permanently asleep on his bed, without any warning. As cruel fate would have it, he had died of a heart attack at just thirty-three years old.

Running the business became secondary and instead, I poured myself into ministry at church. Church became my life. We invested a great deal of time every day, to be at church, running prayer meetings, youth ministries, Christian education planning strategies, worship team practices, women's ministries, bible studies and Sunday School teachings.

You name it, we ran it.

To an onlooker, my involvement may have looked like I was escaping from reality, but to me, it was purely survival and gave my life meaning. The events I'd experienced had been so arduous, not only causing lifelong trauma, but also leading to the ultimate failure of my marriage.

Personal development, or healing self-empowerment, were always high on my to-do list. So, armed with my dreams of higher education and my quest to fulfil this purpose, I continued on the journey. I enrolled in university to pursue a Masters in Public Health. Unfortunately, however, I didn't get very far as our island was ravaged by a savage hurricane.

Hurricane Ivan pretty much left our island akin to a dump heap, with countless people rendered homeless and hopeless. I survived and lived to tell the tale, however, life just seemed to be one struggle after another. Despite overcoming a challenge here and there, I still felt like I was climbing a never-ending uphill mountain, with no peak in sight. I realised something had to change, so I stopped doing what I was doing and took a good, hard look at my life.

In doing so, I noticed I was struggling to be my authentic self.

For years I knew the life I wanted to live but was so afraid of actually living it. I was afraid because I wanted to fit in, but I never wanted to hurt anyone's feelings or cause controversy.

I wanted everyone to feel comfortable around me, never wanting to outshine, just to be safe. I was always afraid I would be victimised; afraid I wouldn't get the things I needed. Afraid to be who I really was, because ultimately, I was a little girl from that tiny Caribbean Island that had to think and behave in a particular way, whatever that was.

I knew in my heart who I was, I knew the kind of life I wanted to enjoy, and I knew I didn't need a lot of money to enjoy the good life.

I KNEW I HAD THE GOOD LIFE.

I was afraid to honor my creator, even though he showed up for me every time and provided what I needed to be, who he created me to be.

I knew who I was, so no one could drag me, or my spirit down, but I was afraid to shine in a world where I allowed money and material possessions to dictate how I behaved, as well as how I responded or reacted to situations I saw before me. I saw myself through the eyes of money and as a result, functioned effectively only when I had money. I realised my self-worth was only determined by the material things I owned or had access to.

Today I thank God for that breakthrough.
I thank God for that release.
I thank God that I am no longer holding on to a limited mindset that says you have to be working for a certain figure to be someone.

That only when you are in that career you can be. That you have to have a particular educational status to be. That one has to be born into a particular family, to be. That you have to be from a particular country to be. That you have to be religious and sanctimonious to be.

Today I am free from this limiting mindset, free from the bind, free from the box, the cage that I allowed people to put me in.

Today I stand proud in my authentic self, celebrating life, accepting myself, loving and accepting people for who they are, but never allowing them to confine me or dictate to me, who they think I ought to be.

Today I say thanks to God for allowing me to truly realise the gem he made in ME and YOU and for embracing the confident, poise, kind, heartwarming, fun loving, hard-working, strong, independent, fierce and powerful woman I am.

Today, I stand in my power, pushing past pain and humbly giving my gift to the world as a healthy powerhouse leader, helping women to break free from limitations, to take their lives back, lose weight, break the sugar addiction, and abandon the martyr mentality and so much more.

After I had come to this realisation, I began to have fun. I continued to teach for a while, but resigned from all other responsibilities, except to exploring new things and experiences for myself and my daughter. I immersed myself in nature, had girls' nights out and went thrift shop shopping for beautiful things, which otherwise I wouldn't have been able to afford.

I dated and enjoyed men.

It was there the real journey of self-recovery and healing started and it was here that I began the process of chasing my dream- owning a business in wellness and wellbeing. I slowly enrolled in wellness classes, such as soap making, massage therapy and more.

I tapped into network marketing and to date, my life as an entrepreneur continues, sometimes winning big and sometimes failing miserably. Taking reckless, and at times, calculated risk, the game of life and business continued. All I knew was that I had a dream of having a business in the Health, Wellness and Wellbeing Industry and as a result, felt I had no choice but to continue in this pursuit.

I valued formal education and given I lived on a small island, moving forward and earning respect was the sensible thing to do. So, I applied for a scholarship to pursue a degree in psychology. I was successful and so the journey continued, this time pursuing a degree full time and trying to build a home-based wellness centre.

This was a rarity where I lived, as most of the businesses in the area were operated by large three and five star hotels, given the island's dependence on tourism. I under-estimated the time, money, patience, and effort it would take to run a profitable business as a divorced woman, with a young child and limited material resources.

The little income I had quickly began to diminish, I had no job, was studying, was earning nothing from the business, was paying rent for both residential and commercial purposes and was also paying private school fees for my daughter. I was either crazy or courageous. I picked the latter. Courage saw me through. The spirit and I aligned. I knew I was unstoppable and had to allow myself to see, and celebrate, success.

My stories are varied and very colourful.

They range from sad, sometimes hilarious, and playful, but always meaningful, filled with value and great wealth. I refused to quit or see myself as nothing short of being a successful Wellness and Wellbeing Entrepreneur. Owning one's power and elevating my business has been tough.

I have had to shift the way I used to think and what I always thought success should look like. I had to be willing to ask for help and take things in my stride.

Restarting, relearning, re-examining, and allowing myself to win was always paramount, and as a heart-centered entrepreneur, I have learned to allow my heart to lead over my brain and see time and money as pure energy.

My concern to people please, allowing glitz and glamour in business to take centre stage, is no longer present. There has been a shift from wanting to survive by pursuing money, to knowing that what I have will always be enough for the right client, and that I do not have to pursue money, because I am my money.

My success in business doesn't depend on the economy, or what is happening around me. Rather, it rests heavily on what's going on inside of me.

Every day I celebrate small wins, using them as bricks to build, allowing my heart to guide me to prosperity. In the words of Dr. Paul

Leon Masters, my silent mentor, "I live confidently each day, knowing that the source of my prosperity is God working through me and directing me." I am unstoppable, my sacred success is guaranteed because I am my money and was built to win.

The old programming of struggle, survival and failure has vanished, and the real program of prosperity, joy and peace has replaced it, bringing inspiration, self-empowerment, and healing, to everyone that crosses my path.

"Always concentrate on how far you have come, rather than how far you have left to go. The difference in how easy it seems will amaze you."

— Heidi Johnson

BE THE GODDESS AND OWN THE ROOM

MARLEY MAJCHER

At times, I think the event planning industry gets a bad rap as a business that, well, is most of the time, solely about partying! But this couldn't be further from the truth, because like any other business, despite my product being 'celebratory fun', I still have profits to make.

I am learning that like most successful business stories, mine also started with a curveball. Following a bad skiing accident, I was forced to rethink my entire life. Rarely do we take leaps without a massive nudge from the universe, and typically, they aren't the best sort of nudges.

They're the ones that leave us feeling dazed, confused, and a little (well, in my case, very) fearful. It was after my accident that I knew I needed to make a big, meaningful change in the form of a new career in the events industry.

Some know me as the party planning and entrepreneurial expert people turn to for all things entertaining. My hard won, failure-based business sense has earned me appearances on various outlets and shows, because I have proven techniques on how to actually make money.

When I wrote my must-read for any entrepreneur, 'But Are You Making Any Money?', I simplified, – in a step-by-step process, – the complicated aspects of running a lucrative business. My profit techniques and conversational style is what Forbes says, "Makes you want to keep reading more."

Among my followers, some would say I have a keen eye for chic trends and clever business techniques to boot, and that this is what makes me a coveted speaker across the United States and around the globe, on subjects such as small business, entrepreneurship, and all aspects of entertaining.

But before we get to the present day, we need to take a giant step back, all the way to when I left my safe and sheltered home of Pasadena, California to head off to Georgetown in Washington, D.C. Unlike many of my GU classmates, I didn't have the aspirations (or the brains) to go into the world of finance or corporate America. I knew, practically from birth, that I wanted to be an entrepreneur.

Before my junior year, I spent the summer in Paris going to cooking school and studying with a French tutor, largely because I didn't have any other bright ideas. When I returned, one of the first assignments I got in my public speaking class was to write on a subject that I knew more about than anyone else. Because everyone was so smart there, my options were very limited. My Mom suggested I do the assignment on French cooking, since there was no way, the other students knew more about that than I.

A few days later, I set off to get my film developed (yes, I am that old), and ran into my professor to whom I blurted out that I had an interview with the chef from 1789. (Which I did not.) She promptly announced that that was her favourite restaurant, and she was thrilled. I was bowled over by my stupidity. Off I went trying to get an interview with that chef.

I got the interview, took one look at him, decided I needed to marry him and then proceeded to work my entire junior year in the bowels of the restaurant. He didn't ask me out, so I quit before senior year, he did ask me out and we were engaged the month after graduation.

If you ever want to see your husband if he's a chef, you'd better get into the restaurant business. We did. He ran the back of the house, and I "ran" - not very well, the front of the house.

When you run a restaurant, handling employees is par for the course, in fact, at one point, I was managing over one hundred staff members. My goal was to do a million dollars in business the first year, which we did, but we also spent a million, one hundred thousand. Not good. I could not figure out how to use all that I learned in business school at Georgetown and apply it to my own business. I thought the problem was not enough volume, so we took over an event space and started a catering company chasing more and more revenue to fix the issues. It didn't.

After many stressful years, we decided to partner up with another restaurant group after I had a bad skiing accident. The writing was finally on the wall for me. The chef and I split (we're still the best of friends) and I went off to start an event planning company, The Party Goddess! I figured that having much lower overhead and barely any employees but myself, I should crush it.

Nope. I ran into the same issues I had in the restaurant business. What threw me off course, again? Simply put, I forgot about actually pricing for profit before I actually sent out a bid. I know that this can sound like an oversimplified statement, and whilst sales are hugely important, if you're not making a profit, then you're not 'in' business, you've got a hobby. And there's nothing wrong with hobbies, but they are different. Being a slave to your business and working every hour under the sun might feel successful, but if the bottom line is looking a bit lean, then is your attention truly in the right place?

Let me reframe, if you're just busy, but you're not making any money, what is the point of being busy at all?

Just because an event planner is booked every weekend, doesn't mean they'll have anything to show for themselves if they aren't laser focused on their margins.

Which leads me to my next point, perception.

I am my own brand and proudly carry the title of, 'Boss of The Party Goddess!', and I have worked ridiculously hard to here. Behind the scenes, I work tirelessly to deliver a premium, albeit quirky service, but I am also a relentless entrepreneur, always looking to improve in my niche. After all, being the authority in your area of expertise is what separates you from the rest. You have to stand out, have unique ideas and a distinct position in the marketplace.

I know everyone from the outside thinks the event planning industry and working with celebrities and jetting off to fabulous locations is super glamorous, and it is, business never stops. I have worked tirelessly for thirty years to get where I am now. There has been a ton of blood, sweat and tears (and more tears), to pull it off and I still can't rest on my laurels.

In our modern-day era of social media everything, we have to keep in mind that just because it appears on your Insta feed, doesn't mean it's real. I've tried to use my social media platforms to show the beauty and excitement of what we do, but also to show the raw underbelly where I fall on my face, and it hurts.

As we know, it's often stepping out of our comfort zone where the magic truly happens. One minute, I had gone from running what looked like an incredibly successful restaurant business, to rerouting my entire career and starting out as an event planner.

Stepping into a new space is always hard, and more often than not, so much harder than we initially realise. I don't quite know how to describe building a business, other than to compare it to childbirth without medication; it's exciting, terrifying, and painful. Kind of like backing into a fan.

As a self-confessed serial entrepreneur, I know the unknown is par for the course, but you've really got to have a very high-risk tolerance, and I had very high goals I wanted to achieve. And that's what I went for.

Enter goal setting.

Having your eye on the prize is as important as having your eye on the profits. Truly, if I had a dollar for every time I rewrote my goals, I'd be living on a private island in the tropics. And I'm still at it. These days, I still write out my goals and visualize them coming true like I'm watching a movie, so they feel real. I try to stay positive, which isn't always easy, but I am tenacious. You can't hit a target you can't see so to accomplish anything you've got to believe in yourself 1,000 percent.

And just as life was rolling along and business was booming, we veered into a global pandemic.

As we know, sprawled across the news, doors were forced to shut, and the hospitality industry ceased to trade. My entire business was hinged on people being in the same room, and with a worldwide lockdown, I went from 'Party Goddess!' to 'Pandemic Panicker'.

Was I going to be flooded in debt?
Was my business ever going to recover?
What did the future even look like?

Despite every fear, I knew that I had the ability to bounce back and respond to the pandemic and come out stronger, despite being in the midst of a global crisis. Let's just say it was incredibly character building. Sure, I shed tears, and lots of them, but successful entrepreneurs are wired to adapt because it runs in our DNA: Change keeps you inventing.

I redid my website, upskilled with new courses, and spent my days connecting with new clients and contacts. Some called me a 'geek', I call it getting off my rump.

These days, any business with which I'm involved has to be focused on the numbers. So, let me share with you some of my profitability hacks I learned along the way:

- Gather a think tank of like-minded business owners to brainstorm ways to reduce overhead and become more efficient.
- Tracking your time is the single most effective thing you can do to turn your company around and put more money in the bank. Period.
- If you suspect that you are leaving money on the table, or working for less than you're worth, it's time to do something about it.
- Make sure you are tracking revenue and expenses for every job to ensure each is profitable.
- When you really pay attention to the hours in your day and how they are actually spent, you're going to be shocked at how much time (translation, money) you're wasting.
- You've got to know (by tracking) the results of your networking so you can choose where to prioritise your networking time. Creating buffers in your pricing to cover unexpected hidden costs is akin to planning for unexpected demands on your time.
- Once you define exactly what you want your work life to look like, you are on the road to success.
- Creating a business plan forces you to face your demons and the underbelly of the business world.

- Reduce overhead. It sounds simple but start by reviewing your recurring expenses and subscriptions that show up every month on your credit card and start hacking away.

As female entrepreneurs, I feel, it's so important to share our successes AND failures with our future peers. There are few greater feelings than saving someone else from a costly mistake you've already paid the price for.

Do you have any aspirations of a life in event planning?

If so, these are for you:

Tips for providing food at events: I think the biggest misconception is that food needs to be fancy. I cannot emphasise enough that it does not. In fact, my thing has always been to do the best that you possibly can for your budget. Meaning, if you say, "Hey listen, I've got $10,000 to spend on catering which really should be $30,000 for the sit-down dinner you're striving for," my philosophy is to totally switch course and pick something completely within your budget. Instead, dig into what other things you like that are inherently less expensive. I love hot dogs, so instead of trying to have some fancy situation I couldn't afford, why not have the most amazing hot dog station that anyone has ever seen in their lives, complete with every topping and bun type under the sun. You get my drift. The point is, do the best, most amazing quality food you can, without trying to be something that your budget just is not.

Volunteers versus outsourcing staff: My recommendation is to cut your budget in other areas, so you can have as many highly skilled staff people as you can afford, who really know what they're doing and can run an event efficiently. It's so tempting to think volunteers can fill in the gaps at an event, but my experience has been that it's not so simple.

Entrepreneurs starting out in the event business: Most of us go into creative businesses or events, because we want to do that thing, right? Whether it's baking cupcakes, or planning parties, or doing flowers, you have to have a really honest conversation with yourself and ask, 'Are you really willing to do all of the other things that every entrepreneur, regardless of how little they're going to make in the beginning, has to do?' If the answer is no, perhaps it's time to rethink your goal and ambitions.

Lastly, I cannot stress this enough, just ask for help.

Whether you are struggling or soaring, going it alone can be, well, lonely. Asking for feedback, thoughts, and even criticism (if you can handle it), provides an opportunity to really up our game. As women, we always encourage our friends and colleagues to open on a bad day but it's rarely something we actually do ourselves. We don't like to burden others; in doing so, we deprive others of the total satisfaction of helping where they can and the knowledge, they themselves will gain. There's an old saying that if you want to learn, teach, and it's so true. I love to explain things to others that I'm good at because it helps me learn even more in the process!

"I am willing to put myself through anything, temporary pain or discomfort means nothing to me as long as I can see that the experience will take me to a new level. I am interested in the unknown, and the only path to the unknown is through breaking barriers, an often painful process."

— *Diana Nyad*

LEAVING YOUR IMPRINT FOR OTHERS TO FOLLOW

KEZ WICKHAM ST GEORGE

My background is in education and the arts, where I majored in Abstract Arts and the Curating of Exhibitions. However, when the joy of the above eventually diminished, it was time to move on and I decided to pursue a more holistic career.

Choosing an education in Aromatherapy, I soon discovered I had a way with words and was encouraged to write monthly contributions, for a newsletter from the Aromatherapy college. This led to writing articles for a local newspaper and a magazine on how the mixing of different oils could ease some ailments of the human body. Once I had completed my diploma in Aromatherapy, I set up a hand and foot massage business. My clients would often tell me their stories. Knowing they considered them to be unimportant was incredibly sad, as my upbringing had been around those who were natural storytellers.

To enlarge my education within the holistic field, I was drawn to Art therapy, where I majored in the specified units of art, philosophy and communication. Here, it was made very clear the importance of storytelling and in particular, its effectiveness when combined with the arts.

I felt my purpose was to integrate my holistic connection, with a small seed of an idea. However, I was unsure if it would open the door to having a palpable business, one which was offering opportunities for artists and authors to see their presence and skills publicly embraced.

To 'read a book by its cover' so to speak is an old adage, however an extremely useful one, especially as I began to put together a vision board for my idea around this very quote. I began by researching the entire South Pacific ring of islands, including New Zealand and Australia, learning that ancestral and multicultural stories were organically blended by intermarriages. It all came down to a genetic code in the art of delivering cultural information, from the DNA of ancestors.

When I was offered a teaching role in (ESOL) English for speakers of a different language, my skills in Art therapy and storytelling proved that most language barriers could be overcome, when we shared stories of our cultures. It was here I began to understand the power of building corridors of communication between many countries, and the power of storytelling, which I had always found fascinating, was beginning to unfold. In particular, I realised that storytelling was not over, instead, it was the human way of leaving our legacy.

Soon, many opportunities to become an author began to present themselves. Firstly, I was offered the position to write a motivation journal for a cosmetic college. When the journal was published, seeing my name in print was an extremely proud moment. I designed myself a simple web page, joining all social media platforms, and before I knew it, vanity publishers began to contact me, their fees outside my original budgets. I also found after reading many contracts, there was a vast difference in the criteria and what they provided.

When I finally found a publisher, who I thought was compatible, I found his values were not aligned with mine. This is important to every strategy in any business, that is, ensuring your values are succinct. I believed his carefully scripted promises, instead of my intuition, and unfortunately, my book was published unedited. Humiliated, I demanded he delete it from his page immediately, knowing it could damage any respect in the literary world for a blossoming author.

When an indie publishing firm in the UK emailed me with a publishing offer, although initially reluctant, we had an informative conversation, following this, I felt our values were in alignment. Collaboration, not competition, was their motto. It proved to be a really successful partnership creatively, but financially, it was disastrous.

Following this, I felt it was time to broach the world of actual book publishing. Knowing this would stretch my finances to the limit, I began by collaborating with others in my field. I had three indie books, plus an instruction manual to my name, and I offered author talks to as many different clubs as possible.

The travel expenses, car maintenance, food and accommodation, proved costly. Although my name as an author and speaker was being spoken about, it was pay as you go. In other words, you pay THEM to speak at their events. I made many acquaintances, but not financial success.

I was convinced there had to be another way, if other authors were finding it profitable to publish, then why wasn't I? Networking meant I was meeting writers, authors, poets, and publishers. For most of them, it was all about making revenue. I was at a loss. I knew I had a great business plan, but to implement it as successful seemed unreachable. It was around this time, I decided to post morning motivation quotes on social media. If I had learnt anything in the years I had spent in the holistic field, it was that our spirit responds kindly to motivation. It proved a popular decision, as I soon gained a small following and also attracted a new publisher. This time, the contract was within my budget and her values were almost akin to mine.

We initially published a trilogy, which proved fairly popular, then a children's book. This particular children's book proved extremely popular, yet the boosting of any sales seemed to fall on my shoulders. I tried an unusual way of promoting, by sending this children's book to the Royal family in the UK, the royal family in Switzerland, as well as the Prime Minister of New Zealand.

They replied, congratulating me. It was an amazing feeling having these formal letters in my hand with the insignias and crests of each Royal House, congratulating me on the authorship of a children's book. I then went to the newspapers, and once again, I found my book in high demand.

When the publisher suggested a book launch in Bali, within the expat community, bookings were made. Once I arrived, there were two book launches booked, one in Ubud, the other in Denpasar. Both launches were very professional, and the attendance was great. However, the sales weren't amazing. In hindsight, this was a blessing, as the tax paid on any sales in Bali was extraordinarily high.

After taking the flights and accommodation, as well as the high taxes into consideration, let's just say it was an expensive holiday. The following year I was invited to Ako, in Japan, as my local community's arts coordinator, which was fully funded by the council, to build relationships between the two sister cities. Here I was offered an opportunity to introduce my children's book. Upon hearing my children's book was being taught as an English lesson in Ako's primary schools, left me with a feeling of absolute joy.

Whilst there, I was offered the position of combining my writing skills, with a well-known Japanese artist, for a short story and poetry novel. The importance of this book was celebrated by both sister cities, and both Mayors spoke of the importance of story telling. Finally, my dream of being an accomplished author was beginning to take shape. I was invited to attend as a speaker at a writer's retreat in Ireland. The interest in authorship there proved to me that storytelling was pivotal to every culture. What authors needed was a sound platform to express themselves. It was an exciting time to explore, and as my fledgling business began to grow wings, everything I had dreamt of was falling into place.

Many writers were looking for somewhere to house their stories, and it was here I was able to offer my services, both as a book coach and book reviewer. Once writers and I had reached agreement and a degree of satisfaction on their outcomes, I would offer them a choice of publishers, which I had become affiliated with. Once they were published, I would then promote their work.

Then Covid arrived and my dream of opening corridors between countries became a struggle. I had to make some challenging decisions; the book reviews and motivational posts on Facebook were still well and truly alive.

However, the coaching side proved unpopular. Success means different things for different people. For me, having a micro business that radiated positivity was essential, but it was also crucial that I found a way to consolidate, with other solid reputations in the world of authorship. Books by the score were being written and published, as with lockdown, people had time on their hands.

The many publishing contracts being offered now included coaching, as well as editing and PR work, hence I became a tiny fish in a noticeably big pond. I realised it was time to recalibrate, this included, not only my own penmanship, but also my self-care and self-support, which were paramount to how I aligned my work and life.

Once more, I began contributing to magazines. Following my instincts, I chose three out of the six that showed interest in my applications. These three were also in line with my own values. Once my contributions proved popular, I was offered the role of structural editor and affiliate in one magazine, plus the opportunity to showcase authors in a book review.

This was an opportunity I did not want to miss, as to advertise or promote myself as an author in these magazines would be advantageous to my business. I then created an author's package for publication, in all three high quality magazines, all with extensive readership numbers.

It was a slow beginning, I watched as other prominent advertisers and promotional firms collaborated with each other, winning business accolades, awards and five-star reviews. My fledgling business was miniscule, compared to the major corporations joining hands. Yet, I had this inner self-belief I had something to offer. My authenticity. I offered an original book review, which was published on many digital platforms, or in one of the magazines, plus it was entered into my book cover awards. Consistent promotion, I believed, was a valuable contribution to any author's career.

Regarding my own manuscript, which was now complete, I was once again looking for a publisher.

This time round, it was one phone call.

The minute we started speaking, she said the words I wanted to hear, "Let's meet and see if we have the same values." Once she had read my manuscript, she suggested I write a trilogy.

Absolutely delighted, I accepted and before I knew it, the contract arrived, my books were edited and proofread, a wraparound book cover was designed and once again, my intuition nudged me to accept her offer. One year later at the book launch the room was packed and I felt overwhelmed.

Finally, I had become a bestseller author overnight. I was walking down that road I had dreamt of, a recognised author.

I was still struggling to sell the package I offered authors, but at the same time, I knew it was too valuable to let go. I knew there had to be a way to make it thrive, all it needed was one publisher to see the value. Then came the launch of the second book in the trilogy, which felt quite different. Although it was well advertised and promoted, the launch was not well-received, particularly as we were experiencing the second wave of Covid. Most of my invited guests decided to stay at home, rather than attend. I read a post on social media citing, "*I had to feel it, to live it, to receive it.*'

This became my mantra.

Taking serious stock of what I had already contributed to the social media and writer's community, it was time for me to accept the offers of travel to join festivals around Western Australia as a storyteller. I was being invited to deliver writing workshops to local shires, and the fact that social and writers clubs wanted to learn the ropes of writing, or to hear my story, made me feel like a success.

An author also then invited me to co-create an anthology with her, sadly I did not check her intentions, aligned or not, or her purpose with this anthology. My intuition flared, but foolishly, I ignored it. I began advertising for co - authors to join us, it took a year to compile the many authors, read their work then semi-edit, it was a stressful tiring job, one I would never undertake again.

The author's stories were captivating and inspiring and as a result, I was inspired to search out a range of promotional avenues, through magazines and television interviews, wanting this anthology to be a number one best seller, not only for me, but for all authors involved, although we made it number 5 on Amazon. Sadly, it proved to be a thankless exercise. Lesson? Listen to your intuition.

Over the years, I continued adding my Morning Motivation posts to Facebook which were proving to be invaluable, I was being invited to speak about mental health and motivation at local radio stations. It was perfect timing, as this led to another opportunity with a festival organiser, and '*Conversations with Kez café*' was born, a creative avenue of promoting the many businesses around Western Australia. My book reviews on radio and YouTube were noticed by an Australian television channel that broadcast to the USA. The CEO rang to invite me to an interview, which I accepted. She commented on my warm and unique interview style, inviting me to a co-host position, which would also involve speaking to authors promoting their work, to an audience of 1.6 million. My world completely opened, my theory was proving to be correct, that publishing a book can be a major catalyst to your success.

Being active across any form of social media gives you huge opportunities, it was obvious I had found my niche when it came to reviews. Offering a free opportunity for all authors, as well as creating my own YouTube channel to showcase these reviews, book reviews came flooding in. Why free? I knew the struggle and the cost I had gone through personally to have my own books reviewed, so I saw this as an opportunity to give back to my writing community and build my name as a professional book reviewer. In the meantime, the publisher I was with, suggested I publish a quote and poetry book, to maintain interest in my authorship and for me soon to be third book of the trilogy.

I did as suggest, launching my poetry book six months later. This book did not do well, a few sales mainly through family and loyal readers, however I saw it as an opportunity, a promotional tool. Another marketing ploy emerged, knowing most of my enquiries were from women, I personally wrapped each book with tissue paper, placed a perfumed business card inside, then posted it. I felt as much enjoyment from the compliments received, as the people receiving them.

My manuscript for book three had been edited and proofed, yet for some reason I could not send it to the publisher. Serendipity was at work. Although, I knew I had something incredibly special to offer my readers, something continued to niggle me. It wasn't until I attended a networking group that I was introduced to a film producer. It was at that moment I knew I was going to have a movie made from this book, which I had called 'Scribe'. It was undoubtedly one of the most courageous opportunities I had ever broached in my entire career. Following up with the producer, she requested to read the prologue.

Two days later, she rang back offering me a contract for a short film that was going to be entered into movie festivals around Australia. A contract between us was signed and I invited all of my magazine affiliates to join me in my new adventure. Fortunately, they were more than happy to use this opportunity for their own promotional push and supported every step of the way.

When 'Scribe' was launched, snippets of the movie were played to attending guests, including a major newspaper editor who subsequently wrote an article on the 'Power of Communication.' I spent a major amount of time promoting both book and movie, knowing this was a crucial component to my career. When the movie premier was advertised eight weeks before opening night, tickets sold out within two days. The actual premier evening was an amazing event, with newspapers far and wide saluting my authorship.

Walking on the red carpet enroute to viewing the movie was such a surreal moment. Photos taken with an Oscar in the background, applause and tributes for my work surrounded me, as not only had I promoted tourism around the city, but also, my actions had brought employment to the area, which in turn, provided the speaking opportunities I was looking for.

Then what?

First and foremost, I needed some self-care, this meant taking time out to refresh and invigorate myself, reviewing my achievements, and acknowledging the hard work I had put into where I stood now.

What do I call enough?

Was I ensuring I worked smart not hard? It became obvious my workload was extensive, so the question was, did I want to remain this busy, or had the time come to cut back a little? I chose the latter.

A four-week travel opportunity was offered, it was here I found the strength and dedication to continue my writing.

Knowing your role in life is an amazing feeling. However, knowing you're helping others achieve their goals, for me, was the goal.

When speaking invitations began to roll in, state and local libraries invited me to talk on the benefits of writing and communication. Writers' festivals invited me to give workshops, and once again, corridors were opening, carrying my message to many. I was even offered the opportunity as a structural editor for an anthology.

When someone fully believes in you and your skills, it's always a time-stopping moment. Can you imagine my delight when this book went to number one best seller in thirty-six countries overnight?

At an author's event, I received an award for my trilogy.

Six months later, another award for my commitment to my writer's community also came my way and I became a finalist in three different awards for leadership.

To author or co-author a book is an amazing passport that opens many doors, like a business card, only more powerful. When you use the title of *'Published Author'* anywhere in the world, it instigates an interest. In retrospect, to become who I am today would not have happened without the opportunities offered and the many friendships I have gained.

My cup is full, to know my contribution has given many authors the opportunity to shine. My advice to all is write your story, join an anthology, and contribute to a newspaper or magazine. Why? Well, why not? To leave your legacy your fingerprint for another to follow.

I will leave you with this quote, *"be seen, be heard, be known"*.

"Destiny is a name often given in retrospect to choices that had dramatic consequences."

— *J. K. Rowling*

A RESONATING SOUND: DHVAANI

POOJA BHATIA

How many times have you imagined yourself as one of the characters while reading a book? Don't we all, at some stage, relate to certain characters? Admire their characteristics? Don't stories open up a new world for us? Since I was a child, I have loved reading books and would often imagine myself as one of the characters.

My all-time favorite character was Scarlet, from 'Gone with the Wind', by Margaret Mitchell. I liked how strong she was and how she coped with trying situations. This is the effect that stories have on us. And this is the very reason I created the platform 'Dhvaani' to share stories about inspirational female entrepreneurs, experts, and ecosystem enablers.

I am an intellectual property (IP) and technology transfer professional, with two internationally recognised credentials, namely RTTP and Certified Licensing Professional. I like to simplify things for professionals and entrepreneurs.

After working for 16 years in the field of innovation, I have now taken a break to explore being a stay-at-home mom, a host and a creator. And yes, I am also an entrepreneur who has created a platform called 'Dhvaani', to showcase the journeys of female entrepreneurs, professionals, and experts, in the field of IP, technology transfer, business and technology. The motto is 'to inspire and get inspired'.

In addition to 'Dhvaani', there are two more platforms that I am working on. One is called the 'Secure, Access, and Apply' abbreviated as SAAply, which curates open calls and funding opportunities for entrepreneurs, startups and innovators.

The other is a mentoring platform to support innovators, aspiring entrepreneurs, and startups, to achieve their dreams. This platform is called 'Investing inTalent', which is in collaboration with Teamstrategize, a partnership firm in India.

I am also an author of a range of books:
Sone Ki Chidiya Ko Jagao, Vol 1., Bridging the gap in innovation ecosystem: Role of Innovation-Technology Transfer Office
Women's Guide to Business Domination, Leveraging Intellectual Property Rights
Magic Weavers:WomeninIP

And I also run a biweekly newsletter on LinkedIn called Voyage, sharing my experience in entrepreneurship, IP and motherhood. I stay connected with the field through these different activities and also through assisting entrepreneurs, startups and innovators, in effectively protecting and commercialising their IP.

How a break turned me into an entrepreneur?

I was working from the United States of America, for the Foundation for Innovation and Technology Transfer (FITT), the IP and Technology transfer arm of the Institute of Eminence: The Indian Institute of Technology, Delhi, heading the IP and technology transfer team. Later, FITT was granted a project from the National Biopharma Mission (a joint initiative of the World Bank and the Government of India), to establish a new Technology Transfer Office (TTO) and I was given the responsibility as the Chief Manager to manage it and bring it to life. The new TTO was named the Innovation-Technology Transfer Office (i-TTO). I hired the staff, trained them, and ran the i-TTO for two years, before leaving the position.

From designing its logo, to curating all of the services, I exceeded myself across every aspect of the project. You could say it was my second baby. Coincidentally, as I took on the position of Chief Manager, my daughter was born in the same month.

> A Technology Transfer Office is an office within the University or Institution which can be part of it or external but caters to the same set of institution. i-TTO was a service TTO serving to many clients not one.

The role came with a number of challenges. Besides working in a different time zone, another difficulty for me was the pandemic, as it disrupted everything, from business development to licensing patents, to generating revenue.

However, I created strategies to steer away from these difficulties and ensure the TTO remained strong and effective. Along with these strategies, standard operating procedures and policies also evolved.

> Key Challenges:
> - Pandemic
> - A disrupted market
> - Market entry was difficult
> - Lack of trained manpower

It wasn't an easy decision for me to quit this job, as I loved what I was doing and had invested all my energy in making it successful. I had complete freedom to implement new strategies, including the way everything operated. However, a simple remark from someone during one of the meetings, where my team was also present, prompted me to rethink my career. So, I decided to leave. Mind you, the remark which changed my destiny, surprisingly came from an unrelated, third party, not even one of my supervisors.

In hindsight, I think it was the right decision, otherwise, I would never have started Dhvaani or SAAply. I had already tasted the thrill of running the TTO as an entrepreneur, so the foundation for my future was already established.

After leaving the job, I took a short break, as I realised, I had been continuously working for 16 years. The first few days were strange, especially given my usual schedule had been thrown out the window.

However, eventually, I began enjoying myself. Even before the end of the three months, things had started to take shape. I had to decide what path to take and turn my ideas into something concrete. As a result, I started Dhvaani, SAAply, collaborated with TeamStrategize, mentored IP and technology transfer professionals, helping startups and innovators. Sometimes, a break can do us the world of good.

Why did I start Dhvaani?

I am often asked why I started Dhvaani and this question always holds a special meaning to me. After leaving my job and taking the three-month break, I was wondering what to do next.

I started talking to my friends about how they manage their day and children, and I found their stories truly interesting and inspiring. It was then I decided to go down a different path and my real journey began. I ran a survey among a few trusted friends, to see how they would react to the idea and whether they were open to being a guest on my show.

Following their overwhelmingly positive responses, I became bolder and began approaching strangers, where to my surprise, the idea was once again well-received. As women, we often don't share the struggles that we face, or how we have managed them. Especially in the field of IP and innovation, there are always deadlines and urgencies, so what does one do to strike the right balance? Do you stop working once you are a mother or fall pregnant? Or do you pursue other opportunities? If so, what?

To address these questions, to inspire other women and to teach them how to learn from their struggles, I created Dhvaani to showcase their journeys. Dhvaani means 'sound' in Hindi, and I wanted this sound to resonate, one that empowers other women. As a result, my platform was born, a platform by women, for women, with the motto, "to inspire and get inspired".

Learnings from the entrepreneurial journey

Being an IP professional and a host are two different worlds, each requiring a different attitude and set of skills. But there are a few similarities too. Both require you to have good communication skills, be empathetic, manage work well, and connect with people. These were the four skills that helped me in the journey of becoming a host. In addition, I chose to stay close to my home turf, that is, IP, entrepreneurship, and innovation.

But there were a number of things that I had to learn:

1. Regarding recording videos, what role does light place in the recording and what equipment to use?

2. How to edit the recorded video and add subtitles to the videos

3. How to grow subscribers for the platform?

4. How to create an interactive website?

I learned all this step by step, slowly like a tortoise. As an IP professional, I wanted everything to be innovative and different, so I even created the soundtrack of my podcast. From the name to the tagline, to the music, I ensured everything was unique and non-infringing.

The most important part of the journey was to set up a process, which I kept refining along the way, and now it's standardised. Creating a content calendar was also critical to ensure there was always content ready to post. I suggest trying new ideas, as you never know what might click with your audience.

I also did not shy away from getting paid tools to help me, such as Canva and Veedio, these two are my best friends. I tried many other tools, before settling on these. If you are wanting to adopt new tools, try them for some time, and use the opportunity of free trials, before committing yourself to one tool.

The last important lesson as a sole team member was to not become overwhelmed by the entire process, to stay motivated, and plan ahead. In the journey of becoming a host, I certainly lost motivation at times, I had conducted interviews, but I could not edit and subtitle them on time, nor post them. I wasn't sure if I was on the right track, but I always had people who boosted me.

So, my advice is, talk to these people, or step aside from what you are doing and experiment. Sometimes, taking a step back helps. I took a step back and started working on a new project, a book-sharing experience of IP Professionals and entrepreneurs: Magic Weavers- Women in IP. This helped me in changing my focus, but I brought Dhvaani back with the book and this has helped me gain momentum.

Key take aways:

- Believe in yourself, if you don't believe in your dreams no one else will.
- Continue learning and expanding your skills. Adding different skills can help you in many ways.

- Grow your network. As someone once said, your network is the net worth. It is worth it, don't shy away from networking.

- Become a member, join or subscribe to various groups and associations. I am a member of the Women's Biz Tribe, and it has really helped me stay motivated by being surrounded by wonderful and inspiring women.

"A woman is the full circle. Within her is the power to create, nurture and transform."

— Diane Mariechild

BREAKING FREE: DISCOVERING YOUR PATH TO SUCCESS

SWATI TYAGI

In the depths of our ordinary lives, there lies an unquenchable thirst for something more—a longing to understand the true purpose of our existence and break free from the chains of societal expectations. This chapter is the story of a woman of colour, from an Indian background, who embarks on an exhilarating journey of self-discovery, defying conventional norms and ending up in Australia.

In this chapter we confront the pressures that society imposes on us, particularly as women, and passionately redefine the true meaning of success. Through introspection and continuous learnings, we uncover the secrets to unlocking our full potential and finding genuine fulfillment, in a world that often tries to confine us.

This is the story of a woman who is striving to decipher the enigma, known as life, to define their own path to success. However, their idea of success may not align with the conventional standards imposed by society. In our everyday life, there is a common belief that a woman is considered successful or fulfilled when she excels in every aspect of life, including being a great mother and having a successful job or career.

I sincerely ask for your unbiased opinion as we explore these questions together. Let's dive deep into our shared curiosity, seeking understanding, without any preconceived notions.

Throughout this chapter, not only am I eager to inspire you, the reader, but in writing this, perhaps I will discover some unanswered questions of my own.

So, here goes!

Decoding the Human Puzzle: Understanding Why We Behave the Way We Do

Q: What factors contribute to the differing behaviours of three children raised in the same environment? Is personality acquired through experiences, or are we born with innate personality traits?

We lived in a small city at our grandpa's house with my mum and two siblings. My dad was a marine engineer, so he was always away due to his work. So, we were kind of raised by our mother.

I was a strong-willed and stubborn teenager, whom everyone considered to be the family's least intelligent child or, the perennial underdog. From the earliest days of my journey, no one held high expectations from me. And oh, the relief it brought! The burden of being the brightest star, the paragon of excellence, or the golden child was lifted from me. And in a strange way, this turned out to be a blessing. I found solace in the fact that no one had high hopes for me.

As I was growing up, I discovered that whenever I tried to be creative or help in the kitchen, things just didn't work out. My mother would get frustrated and yell at me, kicking me out of the kitchen. Cooking was something I couldn't seem to get right, and my family started to see me as someone who couldn't cook. It became a big part of how I was seen within the family. It became clear that culinary skills were not my strong suit.

In contrast, my sister was the epitome of perfection. She was the child who obediently listened to my mother's instructions and eagerly helped with household chores. My sister effortlessly held everything together, smoothly navigating the responsibilities handed to her. As we grew older, our distinct personalities began to solidify even further.

I started to embrace my innate stubbornness and strong-headed nature, and this forged a personality that became my identity. I found myself drawn to outdoor activities, relishing in the freedom of the open air, cycling around purchasing household items from shops. The confines of the indoors could not contain my wild heart, I used to love playing outdoors with my suburban friends.

Being somewhat of an outsider in my own home, my life revolved around the friendships I cultivated, and they held immense significance in my world. I derived great joy from organising events, such as my siblings' birthday parties, where I would go out of my way to find the perfect gifts, even if it meant dipping into my meagre pocket money. These gestures were my way of making others feel special and cherished.

Occasionally, I found myself swept up in moments of theatricality, where my actions defied logic or reason. For instance, if I made up my mind to abstain from wearing traditional Indian attire, no matter how inconsequential the choice may have seemed, I stubbornly stuck to my decision, refusing to waver, even in the face of opposition. It took a firm admonishment from my parents to jolt me out of my obstinacy.

Learning One

Our environment shapes us: What I've learned from the earlier part of my life story is that how people see and expect things from us can have a big impact on our lives, especially in childhood when our brain is still developing, and we are trying to make sense of this world. Without even realising it, I let other people's opinions shape how I saw myself and how I behaved. I held onto the role or identity that was given to me, and my actions were influenced by what others thought of me. It's important to remember that we have the power to define ourselves, and not let others define us.

Let's remember that how we behave, and grow is influenced by many things. We're born with certain traits and qualities because of our genes, but our surroundings, experiences, and choices also shape who we become. It's like a beautiful symphony where nature and nurture come together, making each of us unique and special.

So, let's embrace the complexity of being human, celebrating the different paths we take and the many sides of ourselves. We are born with certain predispositions and traits, but it is through our experiences and choices that we ultimately define our unique personalities. Deep within our individuality, we hold the power to shape our lives, rise above limitations, and discover our incredible potential.

Navigating Parental Advice: Balancing Wisdom and Recognising Imperfections

Are parents always the best advisors, or can they make mistakes too?

In my early years, I was quite headstrong, aggressive, and easily provoked, but deep down, I struggled with feelings of inferiority. Perhaps I masked my anger beneath my tough exterior. My desire was to complete my education and attend a college in a different city. Since I wasn't keen on becoming a doctor like many others, engineering seemed like the logical choice, as everyone around me was going to do it. Following the crowd, I enrolled in an engineering college with the assistance of my father. The college was a boarding school located over 1000 kilometres away.

The prospect of attending an engineering college was both thrilling and daunting for me, as I had always been a pampered and somewhat spoiled child. Not that I didn't know how to share or care, as having siblings teaches you these things. But I wondered what the real world was like and how a small-town person like me would adapt to life in the city, interacting with peers from various backgrounds.

As a child, you tend to absorb everything your parents say, whether right or wrong. Compared to other girls my age, my parents were more liberal, granting us the freedom and rights to pursue our desires. This, in part, fuelled my determination to be a good daughter and never let my parents down. Moreover, I took seriously the unspoken expectation that I should work hard to prove to my father that his efforts in providing me with a good education were not in vain.

Learning 2

The Influence of Upbringing and Environment: The upbringing and the unspoken expectations placed upon me by parents and society greatly influenced my choices and behaviour. The comparison to other children and the belief in working hard to prove my worth, was now deeply ingrained in my mindset. Again, this became my identity.

Should you ease up on yourself and not strictly adhere to every piece of advice given by your parents, allowing yourself to explore and embrace life's experiences while you are young?

At the age of 17, I left my home and never looked back. The first year of college was a rocky adjustment period for me, being exposed to the real world, without the protective shield of my parents. I felt like I was thrown into the deep end, but my independent nature and the support of my friends helped me adapt to this new life relatively easily. This was my initial taste of adulthood, meeting people from diverse cultures and backgrounds, and immersing myself in a variety of traditions and cuisines. Gradually, I began to shed the conservative mentality of my small city upbringing, embracing the excitement of this new life.

Despite being over 1000 kilometres away from my family and having the freedom to do as I pleased, I never felt the need to take advantage of that freedom. Perhaps it was due to the deep-rooted values instilled in me by my parents or most likely, it is my own interpretation of those values. The idea of dating or going out never crossed my mind or seemed enticing to me.

While most of my friends began dating during our second year, I remained cautious and content in my role as daddy's girl. I believed in finding the right partner, informing my parents, and settling down for life. I struggled with a certain degree of inferiority complex or shyness but couldn't pinpoint its origin.

Learning 3

New experiences enhance learning: I discovered a valuable lesson in my later years that embracing a mindset of taking risks, trying new things, and letting go of rigidity can bring immense value to our lives. It is essential to explore different possibilities and seize opportunities when we have fewer responsibilities. Even if we don't realise it at the time, these experiences can lead to personal growth and open doors for learning and self-discovery.

Navigating Life's Uncertainty: Embracing the Present and Living with Purpose

Have you ever noticed how, in moments of uncertainty, we often discover our hidden strengths and shine the brightest when we are thrown into unfamiliar and challenging situations?

Everything was going along smoothly—I had my fair share of mood swings, ups and downs. Academically, I was an average student, neither at the top nor the bottom of the ranks. I was simply following the path of life.

However, everything changed when a major car accident occurred. I broke my femur and spent 4-6 months relying on a walker to get around. The medical advice was to take a semester off to rest and heal, but I refused to accept that.

Learning 4

Life's Unexpected Turns: The car accident I experienced during my college years taught me a profound lesson about the unpredictable nature of life. It reminded me that everything can change in the blink of an eye. This experience made me realise the importance of cherishing every moment and being prepared for the unexpected. It taught me to adapt and find strength, even in the face of adversity.

I vividly remember a lecturer using an example to convince me to take a break: "When a train arrives, not everyone can board it. Some people board now, and others will catch the next one." That example stuck with me, and I decided to defy her advice, continuing my studies and barely passing my exams.

I attended all the practicals and exams while using a walker. My sister, mother, and brother supported me during this challenging time, helping me reach the exam venues so that I could write my papers. This chapter of my life taught me a valuable lesson—life is short, and everything can change in an instant. While it may not have been a life-defining moment, it did change my perspective and how I viewed life. But, as is often the case, time passes, and we tend to forget the lessons life teaches us.

Learning 5

The Power of Persistence: Despite the challenges I faced during my recovery, I chose to persevere and continue my studies. The example of boarding a train resonated with me, inspiring me to keep pushing forward. This experience reinforced the value of persistence and determination. It taught me that with unwavering commitment and hard work, even seemingly insurmountable obstacles can be overcome.

Navigating the Maze of Money

Do you think money is important and can buy happiness to some extent? I am still on the borderline on this one.

I reached my final year of engineering, and some of my friends were involved in serious relationships, while others were considering postgraduate studies or searching for good jobs. I packed up our belongings and sold my scooter, returning to our respective cities to determine the next chapter of our lives.

I was back home, feeling confused about what to do next. Should I start working? If so, where should I find employment? Should I pursue an MBA? Or should I follow my passion at that time, such as attending drama school or becoming an event planner, without worrying about how I would earn money since I had already obtained a degree?

Well, I dabbled in a bit of everything, as many confused graduates do. Eventually, my hunger and ambition took over. Although I wasn't the brightest student, I had always maintained a sense of persistence, willpower, and ambition. I enrolled in a certification course and found myself away from home once again.

During this period, I worked hard and finally secured my first job, which was also located over 1000 kilometres away from home. It was a technical outbound call centre, and the salary was quite attractive. I can still recall the overwhelming feeling of freedom when I received my first paycheck. I didn't quite know what to do with it. That feeling was truly divine. I sent money back home and bought gifts for my friends and family.

This experience introduced me to the world of the rat race, or what I sometimes call, modern slavery. Once you start working, earn money, and become financially focused, there's no turning back. This marked the beginning of my adult life, filled with the pursuit of material success and societal expectations.

Learning 6

Finding Balance in the Pursuit of Success: As we embark on our journey to financial independence, the thrill of earning and providing for our loved ones fills us with a sense of accomplishment. The desire to achieve more and buy gifts for our family and friends can become a driving force. However, it's important to remember that while financial stability is important, it should not overshadow the other aspects of our lives. I didn't realise this at this stage of my life.

Navigating Societal Expectations: The Conventional Path for Children of Diverse Backgrounds

Why are girls from diverse ethnic backgrounds often expected to conform to societal norms and follow a conventional path to appease their parents and society's expectations?

After experiencing different jobs and relocating to various cities in India, the idea of pursuing higher education started taking root in my mind. However, my initial motivation to study abroad wasn't driven by my academic excellence, but rather by my desire to escape the societal pressure of getting married. Allow me to share the backstory behind this decision.

Growing up, like many other children, I had a normal and playful childhood. I enjoyed life and all the things that came with it. The romantic movies and cartoons I watched often portrayed a girl or woman finding her perfect partner and living happily ever after.

Sadly, the society and culture in which we women grew up had ingrained in us the belief that finding "the one" and settling down in a long-lasting relationship was the ultimate goal. It was seen as the key to completeness and success for a woman, alongside education and a career.

The cultural norm dictated that as a girl, you would study, work, and then find a husband, either through your own choice or through arranged marriage. Once married, the expectation was to bear children and have a lifelong companion. This was considered the conventional path that everyone followed.

As I entered adulthood, I was constantly reminded of the expected behaviours for a woman. I was told not to be aggressive or stubborn, as it wouldn't align with the ideal image of a wife. I was encouraged to be adaptable and accommodating, to learn how to cook, and to fulfill the role of a caregiver for my future husband and his family. The list of societal expectations seemed never-ending.

Amidst completing my undergraduate studies and exploring various short to medium term jobs, the topic of marriage started to arise. People would often ask me about my thoughts on marriage, as proposals were being offered. This question sent shockwaves through my wild heart, which was yearning to achieve what my parents had sacrificed. Being naive at that time, I couldn't handle the question from my dad, and I ended up not speaking to my father for months, utterly shocked that such a question was asked of me.

Learning 7

Women should have the freedom to challenge societal expectations and pursue their own goals, even if it means going against traditional norms of marriage and finding a life partner.

Navigating Uncharted Territory: Moving Overseas

Why do we have to follow a conventional path? Who creates these rules in society, regarding what is wrong and what is right?

With the completion of extensive paperwork and a daunting process, I finally decided to set my foot in Sydney, Australia. Although my parents were always supportive of my decisions and encouraged me to pursue education and personal achievements, my motive for choosing post-graduation was to escape the looming pressure of marriage, a fear that still lingered within me due to my independent and single lifestyle.

With a heart filled with anticipation and a mix of nerves, I took my seat on the plane—a seat that would transport me to an entirely new chapter of my life. This wasn't just any flight; it was my first time flying internationally, and the magnitude of the journey sank in. As the plane soared through the skies, I couldn't help but feel a sense of both excitement and trepidation.

Arriving in Australia, I found myself in a foreign land, surrounded by unfamiliar faces. Except for one distant friend from college, I didn't know a single soul. The realisation hit me that I was starting anew, once again transitioning from being a working graduate, to becoming an international student. I felt a whirlwind of emotions, a fresh start that held immense promise and potential.

As I embarked on this incredible adventure, I quickly learned that adapting to a new culture, grappling with a different accent, and navigating unfamiliar ways of operating, would be a significant learning curve. It required me to step out of my comfort zone and embrace the unknown with open arms. The days were filled with thrilling moments of exploration and discovery, as well as the challenges of balancing my studies and finding a part-time job.

Amidst the excitement and challenges, I couldn't help but feel a surge of passion coursing through my veins. This new chapter of my life was a canvas waiting to be painted with vibrant hues of experiences and personal growth. Every interaction, every encounter, and every triumph or setback became a part of my journey, fuelling my determination to carve out a place for myself in this foreign land.

Yes, it was undeniably both exhilarating and challenging, but that's what made it more worthwhile. It was in those moments of uncertainty and stepping into the unknown, where I discovered a strength within me, I never knew existed. It was a transformative experience, shaping not just my academic path, but also molding the very essence of who I am today.

As I embarked on my journey, juggling university and two part-time jobs, my determination to earn money and establish independence was unwavering. Moving to Australia meant starting from scratch, as overseas experience held little relevance here. While my friends indulged in dating and thoughts of settling down, I immersed myself in work, unaware of how they were gradually entering matrimonial bliss one by one. My sole focus was on accomplishing my goals of financial stability and making my parents proud.

Learning 8

Finding Personal Identity: Moving away from home and experiencing life in a different city allowed me to break free from the confines of my conservative upbringing. It was a period of self-discovery and financial growth. I learned to question societal expectations and explore my own passions and desires. This journey taught me the importance of staying true to oneself, following one's dreams, and not simply conforming to the choices made by others. It emphasised the significance of individuality and finding one's own path in life.

However, a fallout with my childhood best friend, upon whom I was emotionally dependent, turned out to be a blessing in disguise. It set me on a path of self-discovery and taught me the importance of not relying solely on one person. Along this journey, I forged new friendships, while some of my old ones faded away. I discovered spirituality, which provided me with strength, wisdom, and a renewed sense of connection and purpose in life.

Amidst these personal developments, the pressure from my parents to get married remained constant. They, too, faced societal scrutiny and had to answer probing questions from people back home about why their daughter was still single. Every phone call and trip back home became an emotional ordeal for me, as I knew deep down I wasn't ready for marriage. Despite the relentless pressure, I stood firm in my decision and refused to succumb to societal expectations. My resilience served as my armour.

Upon the request of my parents, I was on matrimonial websites for a while, but the incessant questions about being the ideal wife, such as taking care of in-laws, cooking, smoking, and drinking, frustrated me. Although I possessed the qualities that fit the mold perfectly, I refused to prove my worthiness to someone else to get their, "Yes".

Learning 9

Breaking the Mold: Challenging Societal Expectations as a Woman of Colour: The journey of self-discovery and staying true to oneself, even in the face of societal pressure and expectations, is essential for personal growth and fulfillment. It is important to listen to one's own desires and values, rather than conforming to external norms and judgments, to lead a meaningful and authentic life.

Redefining Yourself Through Setbacks: How One Moment Can Reshape Your Life

Do you believe that everything happens for a reason and that every negative experience teaches us valuable lessons?

Years passed in my quest to find a suitable partner, and although I was content in my own happiness, the nagging thought of disappointing my parents lingered in my mind. To compensate for my perceived deficiency in the realm of personal relationships, I focused on building my financial independence, investing time and energy in acquiring properties and making wise financial choices to fulfill my parents' dreams and define my own version of success. I diversified my investment portfolio, exploring opportunities in properties, stocks, ETFs, and more. This became my driving force.

Simultaneously, in the background, I cautiously embarked on the search for the perfect life partner, though my enthusiasm was tempered by a lingering skepticism that such an ideal match truly existed outside of fairy tales. I was doing this for the sake of societal pressure.

Finally, I encountered someone who seemed to fit the bill, and my hopes soared. We shared common interests, and everything appeared to fall into place. The happiness around me was palpable, but unfortunately, things didn't work out as expected. The shattered expectations and heartbreak left me feeling disheartened and my confidence took a hit.

Rejection is never easy to bear. Yet, upon reflection, I am grateful for this experience, despite the sadness it brought. It has shaped me into a different person. It became clear that I was not yet equipped to handle a relationship, lacking the necessary experience, and it cost me dearly. Nevertheless, I have come to understand that every experience serves a purpose and contributes to personal growth.

Introspection and self-reflection became my daily companions. Month by month, I dedicated myself to becoming a better version of myself. Personal development became an ongoing practice, and I witnessed remarkable changes within me. I began to engage in enjoyable activities and embrace life more fully. I tried many new activities which I would not have tried before.

This experience also shifted the dynamics with my parents, as they realised the futility of forcing me into something that may not be destined for success. They recognised that my happiness should be the ultimate goal, as it is I who would bear the consequences of any missteps. In the end, all that truly matters for us as humans, is to live life authentically and find our own happiness.

Learning 10

Happiness comes from within: It is important to invest in personal development, engage in introspection, and pursue activities that bring joy and fulfillment, ultimately prioritising one's own happiness rather than conforming to societal expectations, due to cultural barriers.

Navigating the Tug-of-War: Guilt, Work, and Home in the Life of Migrant Kids

Why do migrant kids often feel guilty when moving abroad and being unable to support their parents ? Why do we constantly find ourselves torn between our home country and our work land? Is it possible to strike a balance and have both?

In the midst of a comfortable job and a decent income, I find myself yearning for something more, as if there is an inherent restlessness within me that drives me to seek answers to profound questions. I have consciously chosen an unconventional path that deviates from societal norms, embracing a single independent lifestyle. Yet, despite this intentional choice, I cannot help but question why I remain confined to a single city, when my true passion lies in travelling, exploration, and being there for loved ones.

Also, every day, as an immigrant, the longing to be present for my parents and share meaningful moments with them, weighs heavily on my heart. However, the constraints imposed by a nine-to-five job often obstruct my ability to honor that deep-rooted commitment. I am certain that this inner struggle resonates with the minds of countless immigrants, as we grapple with the delicate balance between our professional obligations and the cherished bonds with our loved ones.

The fear of depleting my savings casts a shadow over my thoughts, as it threatens to overpower my desires and aspirations. Why does it feel so elusive to discover our purpose, or pursue our dreams and passions? When will I finally uncover that elusive sense of purpose and passion that will bring clarity and fulfillment to my life? These are the profound musings that swirl within me, urging me to embark on a journey of self-discovery and seek the answers that will shape the course of my life.

Learning 11

Prioritising Meaningful Connections: Sometimes, choosing to prioritise personal relationships, such as spending time with parents, can bring more meaning and fulfillment than indulging in leisurely travel. Recognising the importance of nurturing family bonds and making them a priority, can lead to a deeper sense of fulfillment.
I am still trying to seek answers to some of the questions raised above.

Embrace Life: Discovering Happiness and Independence Beyond Societal Expectation

As I move towards the final few thoughts and paragraphs of this chapter, I would like to share something with you that has become so much clearer for me.

DON'T STOP YOUR LIFE WHILE WAITING OR SEARCHING FOR THE RIGHT ONE, DUE TO SOCIETAL OR PEER PRESSURE. DATE YOURSELF FIRST AND FIND HAPPINESS WITHIN, THAT WILL GUIDE YOU TO CARVE YOUR PATH. Whether that is being alone or being with someone.

I have more time to look after social causes or things I care about. I have more time to be social, spend time with friends, try activities I enjoy, and learn new things.

You do not need one romantic connection to feel a sense of belonging. Instead, you have time to spend with friends and parents and learn and grow a lot as part of this process. That has always been my mantra: Not relying on romantic relationships to feel complete.

Being single gives you freedom and autonomy. For example, you get to do what you want to do as per your values. You live a more meaningful and purposeful life.

Conclusion: Create Your Legacy

This is my life and my message to you.

Don't let anyone judge you. You are perfectly normal. Being single is ok and has its positives. Your only goal is to be yourself; it all depends on what you like to do and at which stage of life you are.

Be bold.
Wear your single status with pride.

It's time to push the pins on things that matter to you and not to others, own up to yourself, stand by your wishes and dreams, tall and proud, courageous, and unfazed.

Define and stick to what being single means to you – It means freedom from expectations, commitment, no fear of heartbreak, invasion of privacy, achieving your goals, learning new things, traveling, or looking after and being there for your parents.

I have made that choice and I am happy with it. So, whoever you are, be sure it's your choice and work to be happy, live to be exuberant, and breathe to be lighter.

For now, I am single. Who knows, it may or may not change. But who cares, as we won't waste any minute of this precious life doing what we aren't meant to do, nor listening to our hearts.

I've been thinking a lot about the challenges that single people face, especially when they reach old age, experience health issues, or feel lonely. I want to make a difference by advocating for their rights and creating a safe space, where single women can find support and security.

It's interesting how my parents always questioned me about the future, asking what I would do when I'm older, fragile, and alone. But you know what? I believe that being single doesn't mean being helpless. I want to find the answers to those questions and show everyone that we can take care of ourselves, even in challenging times.

Another thing I'm excited about is exploring a location-independent lifestyle. The idea of having the freedom to live and work from anywhere is so enticing, but I admit, there's also a bit of fear regarding stability creeping in. Nevertheless, I'm determined to push past these concerns and embark on this journey of self-discovery.

I'll be sharing updates and experiences along the way, so stay tuned! Let's come together and support each other on this quest called life. Join me as we navigate the ups and downs of life and embrace the beauty of being independent.

> *"The question isn't who's going to let me; it's who is going to stop me."*
>
> *— Ayn Rand*

SEIZE THE MOMENT, EMBRACE SUCCESS

ANNIE GIBBINS

Would you believe it? I'm writing this final chapter of "Memoirs of Successful Women" on a plane, travelling back from Melbourne. During my brief visit, I found myself sitting with some girlfriends, savouring a delightful seafood lunch in the bustling backstreets of this urban paradise. Today, I am filled with happiness. This word holds great significance for me because feelings are fleeting, and life is unpredictable.

Happiness is something I value immensely.

I hope my children and grandchildren experience as much happiness as possible. I hope my husband remains joyful as we embark on our thrilling journey through life. I hope my clients feel elated as they achieve their goals. And I hope you, dear reader, find happiness as you glide over the final pages of this book, knowing that my co-authors and I have provided you with everything you need.

As I reflect on the stories within this beautiful anthology, I am reminded of the one constant in life: change.

Curiously, or rather magnificently, we humans love to daydream about change. Yet, when alternative paths present themselves, change can unsettle even the most steadfast individuals. We are paradoxical beings, prone to introspection.

We delight in painting mental pictures of the perfect life, but when it comes to taking action, fear often paralyses us.

Fear is a peculiar thing—not humorous, but rather odd.
It is often linked to our ego: What will people think of me? What if I fail? What will happen if I succeed?

Trust me, these fears are genuine, especially for those who lack self-belief. However, let me pose this question: "What would you rather feel: fear and success, or just fear?"

It seems that, for the most part, we humans have a tendency to live in the future, constantly planning and envisioning events and experiences that may or may not come to fruition. It's a curious phenomenon considering that, in reality, we don't possess any magical powers that allow us to control the future beyond the present moment. While we can make arrangements, book holidays, and organise weddings, there's no guarantee that any of these plans will actually materialise.

Nevertheless, we persist in planning.

This inclination stems from our innate desire to shape our lives, pursue our dreams, and find a sense of security and purpose. Planning allows us to set goals, establish a sense of direction, and work toward the future we envision.

It provides us with a framework within which to make decisions, allocate resources, and take actions that increase the likelihood of achieving our desired outcomes.

While it's true that the future is uncertain and plans can easily be disrupted, the act of planning itself serves multiple purposes. It helps us clarify our aspirations, identify potential obstacles, and consider alternative courses of action.

Through planning, we become more intentional and proactive in shaping our lives rather than passively letting circumstances dictate our path. Moreover, the process of planning brings anticipation, excitement, and hope.

It allows us to imagine the possibilities that lie ahead and cultivates optimism and motivation. Even if our plans don't unfold exactly as we envisioned, the act of planning often leads to valuable experiences, personal growth, and unexpected opportunities along the way.

So, while there are no guarantees in life, planning serves as a powerful tool that empowers us to navigate the future with purpose and intention. It helps us strive for the life we desire, adapt to changes, and make the most of the present while preparing for what lies ahead.

And speaking of love...
Let me share a story about my dear friend, Nina.

She is a successful businesswoman with an impressive resume. However, what she truly yearned for was her own love story. She would go on occasional dates and chat with interesting individuals online, but deep down, she never believed she would find new love after her painful divorce. She shielded her heart with her analytical, business-oriented mind, strategising her emotions—an aspect of ourselves that longs for a more carefree existence. Yet, strategise she did.

One day, unexpectedly, Nina met a man while both were waiting at a bar to order pre-theatre drinks. They exchanged smiles, as people do, but thought nothing more of it. Nina had become convinced that meeting someone in person was a rarity in the age of dating apps and blind dates arranged by well-meaning friends.

However, this handsome "silver fox" simply said, "Hello." It wasn't a chat-up line with an ulterior motive; it was a simple, harmless, innocent gesture. Fast forward two months, and Nina is planning her first weekend getaway with this intriguing stranger she met at the bar.

After exchanging phone numbers and spending countless hours chatting on the phone until the early morning hours, Nina can't believe how happy she feels. However, her fears begin to cloud her mind, causing her to strategize her way out of the fear of potential disappointment. What she fails to realise is that her success story is unfolding before her very eyes.

You see, my friend, I am an entrepreneur through and through. I sleep only six hours a night, work across multiple time zones, and conduct business from anywhere imaginable—Nepalese mountain tops, for instance.

I dedicate my attention to all that is important to me.

I am driven to succeed in my various ventures because I desire financial security, aspire to build a global community of female leaders, and wish to educate young women and girls that anything is possible. I remain open to every plot twist that life throws my way.

With the right mindset toward money, mindful ambition, and effective communication of your personal brand, I can assure you that success is waiting for you. Remember, success is not just an abstract concept or a dated snapshot of what it once was. We are no longer defined by stereotypes, assumptions, or clichés. We no longer have to apologise for wanting more.

We are no longer limited to fighting poverty among women; we now have the ability to address this issue in innovative and unique ways. Somewhere, someone before us was a woman who desired to challenge the status quo and bring about real change. This change may occur within the confines of a family home, a village, or even an entire country. There are girls sitting in classrooms right now who will become future leaders, and they rely on us to widen the path for them.

We have communities that can learn from us, heal through our knowledge, and empower themselves to grow and flourish. We have business conglomerates that need our emotional intelligence. No longer are we labelled as "oversensitive"; instead, we are seen as passionate and vibrant. We are not abandoning our domestic roles; we are reclaiming our futures.

The world is in desperate need of compassionate guidance and a clear vision, and guess what? We can deliver both. We can exceed expectations, raise our voices, run swiftly, and build towering achievements.

We can. And we will.

It's easy to become entangled in the routines of life. Yes, some routines are simple and mundane—taking the kids to school, preparing dinner, paying the mortgage—while embodying the role of a wonder woman day in and day out. We are partners, mothers, daughters, sisters, colleagues, and friends.

In the blink of an eye, so much can change, and time can slip away. However, let me assure you that igniting a sense of spontaneous urgency is not my intention. Knee-jerk success building is not for everyone, and the last thing we need is more burnout from trying to fulfil the expectations placed upon us as women.

Instead, I want to leave you with this empowering message: Live your life on your terms.

Living life on your terms doesn't necessarily mean packing up your belongings and trekking across the Sahara Desert (although if that sounds appealing, start packing!). It starts with taking small actions, one step at a time. You don't have to be reactive to find happiness, and you certainly don't have to wait for a cosmic sign to push you forward. Remember, money can be helpful, but it's not the key to true happiness.

Sometimes, it may feel like hours drag on and lifetimes pass by, leaving us wondering how to make the most of each moment. There's a saying I love: "Those who don't have time for meditation need it the most." It's a powerful reminder.

Even if you have little time in your day, if you can't spare two minutes to write down one action that will bring you closer to success, then my friend, when you reach this very last page of the book, I urge you to pause. Don't move. Don't reach for your phone.

Just sit still, take a deep breath, and ask yourself this question: "What step can I take at this very moment towards my success?"

Repeat this question and let it resonate within you. Feel the motivation, the determination, and the power that lie within your answer. Success is not a distant dream—it is within your reach, waiting for you to take action.

So, my fellow women, seize the moment, embrace success, and live your life your way. Trust in your abilities, lean on your strengths, and believe that you have the power to create the life you desire. Remember, you are not alone on this journey. We are here, supporting each other, breaking barriers, and building a brighter future for ourselves and generations to come.

Now, my friend, close your eyes, take that moment of stillness, and envision the path to your success.

When you open your eyes, take that first step. The world is waiting for your extraordinary contribution.

"You never lose by loving. You always lose by holding back."

— *Barbara De Angelis*

ABOUT THE AUTHOR

Annie Gibbins is a true Renaissance woman, with accomplishments in every facet of the business world. As an acclaimed TV and podcast host, keynote speaker, #1 best-selling author, publisher, and business mentor, Annie has established herself as a leading voice for women in business. Despite her numerous accomplishments, Annie's story is one of resilience and determination. She has successfully raised a family of five, including two sets of twins born only 26 months apart, all while building an incredible 7-figure business empire. Through Women's Biz Global, Annie has mentored countless women from around the world, helping them to achieve their goals and reach their full potential by calling out limiting beliefs, clarifying purpose, and developing strong business practices. Annie's story is a shining example of the incredible heights that can be achieved with hard work, dedication, and the right mindset. Her journey inspires women everywhere to break down barriers and achieve their wildest dreams.

Heidi Dugan is a living, breathing and inspiring story of success. An entrepreneur, celebrity TV host, wellness advocate and media darling, are just some of the terms used to describe her. Having lived in China for almost 30 years, she became the first foreign TV host to have her own TV show in China, which reaches over 6 million viewers daily, is a live host on Oriental Shopping channel, completing up to $2 million in sales in one and a half hours. Heidi is a highly sought after ambassador and adviser to foreign brands, focusing on health, wellness, beauty, and food and beverage categories, and leverages her experience and influence across a wide range of online and offline platforms. Heidi has received awards such as Best Foreign TV Host and Most Popular Foreign TV Host, International Leading Woman in Business of the Year, International Alumnus of the Year, and Australia China Alumni Award for the Arts and Creative Industries. As Director of Arete Group, Heidi offers companies and brands strategic advantage to successfully integrate into the community, connect with the consumer, and ultimately build their business faster in China, one of the largest economic markets in the world. Her influence across Australia and China has been recognized through her media coverage on Channel 9 news, Australian Financial Review, Harper's Bazaar, China Daily to name a few. Through her brand *RIZE This is Living*, She partners with brands, the

Chinese Government and Shanghai Women's Association to better educate and train woman in health, wellness and career development.

For over 25 years, Suzy Michael's expertise and work in media have encapsulated different platforms, specifically broadcast television, broadcast radio, podcast, print, streaming and various online forms. Suzy's career and experience include television presenter, journalist, television producer, news anchor, print editor, podcaster, radio host and national media manager. Suzy's passion and integrity are evident in her broad portfolio of work. She is known for her international work as a broadcast television host and executive producer, where she has presented and produced a wide range of genres, including lifestyle, news, biographies, and entertainment. Her expertise in these areas has earned her a reputation for being a highly sought after woman, and she has worked with major media outlets across the globe. Known as *the voice people trust*, Suzy has a unique talent for captivating audiences and leaving a lasting impact. Suzy's ability to bring out the heart of a show has earned her a reputation as a compelling television presenter and producer. Born in Australia with Egyptian heritage, Suzy is in high demand for her charming and authentic presenting style. Her style is current, inspiring, and captivating. Her fresh and bubbly approach instantly connects with the audience, enabling high quality content and entertaining media. Suzy is well-known in the Australian community and has interviewed many prominent names across Australia and the globe. She has a keen interest in lifestyle, entertainment and investigative journalism and is dedicated to bringing purposeful entertainment to the screens. As a runner-up for the *Young Australian of the Year Award* in 2000, Suzy has progressed with the changing tides of media, and her star power is still rising. She has worked closely with various media channels, businesses, educational institutions, and community groups. Throughout her many years in media, Suzy is known amongst the local, national, and international community as being a vibrant woman who forms instant connections and brings engaging content to her audience. Suzy is a highly respected media specialist with a career that highlights her significance and abilities in television. Her magnetism and zeal exude charisma on-set as she entertains and builds rapport with her audience. She provides interesting, valuable, passionate, compelling and most of all, enjoyable content for all ages in every country.

Shelli Brunswick, COO of Space Foundation, brings a broad perspective and deep vision of the global space ecosystem — from a distinguished career as a space acquisition and program management leader and congressional liaison for the U.S. Air Force to her current role overseeing Space Foundation's three primary divisions: Center for Innovation and Education, Symposium 365, and Global Alliance. Advocating for space technology innovation, entrepreneurship, diversity and inclusion, Shelli collaborates with organizations around the world to connect commercial, government, and educational sectors. Shelli was named the 2022 Chief in Tech of the Year, 2021 Global Technology Leader and the 2020 Diversity & Inclusion Officer and Role Model of the Year Award by WomenTech Network. Shelli plays an active leadership role with United Nations Office of Outer Space Affairs Space4Women, WomenTech Network, World Business Angels Investment Forum (WBAF) Global Women Leaders Committee (GWLC) Co-lead, G100 Global Chair for Space Technology and Aviation, Global Policy Insights – Global Policy, Diplomacy and Sustainability (GPODS) Fellowship program, Global Policy Insights -- Quad Forum, Space Tourism Society Africa, Tod'Aérs, Lifeboat Foundation, America's Future Series, Women's Global Gathering, Manufacturer's Edge, and Colorado Springs Chamber & EDC.

Patricia Jo Grover, The Goal Achievement Strategist, incites action with the platform that she specifically created around her proprietary "Conquering Skills Education" to Encourage, Educate, and Empower individuals to achieve more success and be able to "Rise Above" any Challenges they may have in any of the 8 Dimensions of Life. She uses a heart – centred approach, that focuses on helping her clients have Mindset Shifts, create New Belief Windows, and find their Why and Purpose. Allowing them to Dream, Conquer Fears, and Create a Work/Life Balance so they can Have, Be, Do, and Earn more while they live their lives Purposefully, Joyfully, and Gratefully. her 30 years of Business In Management & Ownership, she has recruited, trained, coached, consulted, taught, and mentored over 3500 Entrepreneurs, Corporate Employees, and Staff of her own businesses. And is now working on her Ph. D in Entreprenology at the International University of Entreprenology.

Layne is regarded as one of the world's most successful athletes. 19 years on the pro tour. 7 world titles. The only surfer in history, male or female, to win six consecutive world titles. 5 won in a state of fear. 2 in a state of love. Beyond the world titles, beach lifestyle, celebrity status, and rockstar husband, Layne's story is one of overcoming significant obstacles in and out of the water including Chronic Fatigue syndrome, depression and family loss. Navigating her way through success and failure, Layne is a champion for mental wellness, believing our fears, setbacks and limitations are a hot spot for growth and opportunity. Since retiring from professional surfing, Layne has channelled her intensity of a 'tiger shark' to continue fighting for causes close to her heart. Protecting the oceans and all that lives in them as a passionate environmental campaigner, paving the way as Chair of Surfing Australia, supporting people through their mental health challenges as ambassador for Black Dog Institute and RUOK? Day, and empowering humanity to develop its mental and emotional well-being via her Awake Academy. As a highly sought-after motivational speaker, workshop facilitator and presenter, Layne is driven to awaken a groundswell of centred, connected, and confident people to design a life they love. Layne's no bullshit approach to life and leadership is refreshingly real, straight to the point, moving, funny and highly applicable to people in all walks of life. She surfs every day, loves Rosé and her biggest weakness is hot chips.

Reverend Joslyn Farray Pierre, The Intuitive Wellbeing Educator is an Ordained Minister, Metaphysician, Integrative Nutrition Health Coach, International Award Public Speaker, and Author. A proud mom of two, one since passed. Her work as an Educator and Administrator within the Caribbean, spans over 3 decades in Grenada & Trinidad and Tobago. She is an Ambassador of Peace, Health, Wellness and Wellbeing to several local and international NGOs and a member of Grenada Published Authors' Association. Rev.Joslyn's focus is to be of service to women teaching, coaching and counselling through her Self-Empowerment and Sacred Self-Care programs; helping women to take control of the (WPW) weight, plate, and wealth in their lives, from, anxiety, weight loss to healing trauma, taking care of their mind, body and spirit, helping them to experience wholeness, living a lifestyle of joy and fulfilment.

Marley Majcher is the CEO of The Party Goddess!, a nationally acclaimed full-service event planning and catering company, and author of 'But Are You Making Any Money?', a witty and lauded business guide for entrepreneurs. From understated elegance to rock star fabulous, Majcher is known for creating the most talked about parties of the year for a client list ranging from top-tier businesses to A-list celebrities such as Pierce Brosnan and Sofia Vergara, but she is quickly establishing herself as one of the best resources for small business owners and entrepreneurs. Heralded as a must-read for any entrepreneur, Majcher's book, 'But Are You Making Any Money?', simplifies — in a step-by-step process, the complicated aspects of running a lucrative business. Her pricing strategy, profit technique and conversational style is what Forbes says, "makes you want to keep reading more." Majcher is the party planning and entrepreneurial expert people turn to for all things entertaining. Her popular savvy and business sense have earned her appearances on various outlets and shows including "Fox and Friends," Fox Business, MSNBC, "Extra," "Good Day LA," Bravo, E!, MTV, HGTV, FOX, ABC, CBS, NBC and The Wedding Channel. Majcher has championed her unique approach to events and inspired many to create lasting memories through her featured articles and interviews in publications such as *The Wall Street*

Journal, Fortune, Us Weekly, People, OK!, Marie Claire, Women's Day, In Style Weddings, Business Week, Entrepreneur Magazine *and* The Robb Report, as well as multiple radio interviews including Martha Stewart's Sirius Radio show. Her keen eye for chic trends and clever business techniques has made her a coveted speaker across the United States and around the globe, on subjects such as small business, entrepreneurship, all aspects of entertaining and her celebrated coaching programs. Majcher's beloved presentations challenge entrepreneurs to not only think outside the box but to forget a box even exists. Majcher has also contributed to several books, including "It's Your Business: 183 Essential Tips that Will Transform Your Small Business", by JJ Ramberg, host of the MSNBC show "Your Business." She also writes for various publications including Entrepreneur.com. She has received many honors and awards, including the Chamber's Entrepreneur of the Year Award three years in a row, was named an Outstanding Young Woman of America and has been honored by the State of California as a Small Businesswoman of the Year. Majcher earned a degree in marketing with a focus on entrepreneurship from Georgetown University's McDonough School of Business, where she returns to guest lecture annually. She regularly participates in the university's webinars and events in Los Angeles, New York City and Washington, D.C. Majcher currently spends any free time she might have, usually between 10:45 p.m. and 11:15 p.m. on Tuesdays, with her three very naughty children.

Kez Wickham St George is a highly gifted writer Professional. A bestselling award-winning author, recently winning a gold Titan award, she has recently been invited to speak at the NSW state Library, a women's summit Bali plus Ireland at Crom Castle. Kez is the global writer's consultant and a book coach, who is very passionate about championing people from diverse backgrounds to tell their stories and write with passion. As a leader in her profession, she has spoken nationally and globally, sharing her wisdom and knowledge about the process of writing, editing, and producing all forms of written communication. Kez contributes to a number of regular magazines, sharing her insights. She has also coordinated and compiled a number of anthologies. Across her Western Australian community, she is known for her work empowering people to write, heal with art therapy, and gives back via her volunteer work. Kez has co- produced and co-hosted a weekly international show, highlighting the work of authors and artists across the world. She has since gone on to produce a short film from the prologue of her last novel Scribe, shown across theatres in Australia. Kez is consistent and dedicated along with her incredible creative energies and refreshing idealism.

Pooja Bhatia, Chief Executive Officer, Inoberry LLC wears many hats from a strategist, a host, an author, and a creator to a mom. She has 17 years of experience in Intellectual Property, technology transfer, patent licensing, and policy. Pooja holds an MBA degree in Technology Management, and two internationally recognized credentials: Certified Licensing Professional, and Registered Technology Transfer Professional. She helps entrepreneurs, startups, and academics in IP management and commercialization. Pooja also mentors young professionals, entrepreneurs, and technology transfer offices on IP-related matters.

Swati Tyagi is a dynamic and ambitious global management consultant with a passion for leveraging her expertise in the tech space to tackle complex challenges through effective collaboration. With an extensive professional journey spanning decade, Swati has excelled in various areas, including digital product delivery, information management, data warehousing, and reporting, across diverse industries in Australia, India, and Europe, including telecommunications, finance, transportation, and the ICT sector. But Swati isn't just about business and technology; she firmly believes in the power of attitude, compassion, and caring. She knows that with the right mindset and determination, anything is possible – in both work and life. Driven by a deep-rooted belief in the power of attitude, compassion, and care, Swati embraces life with a purpose-driven approach. In her professional journey, Swati has always focused on understanding others' needs and using tech to make their lives easier. That passion for helping others spills into her personal life too. She's on a mission to create a vibrant community for single, independent women where they can see being single as an opportunity and not a curse. Swati firmly believes that being single does not equate to loneliness but offers the freedom to explore passions, chase dreams, and connect with like-minded souls who uplift and inspire each other. In her chapter for this anthology,

Swati shares her incredible experiences, wisdom, and insights, inspiring readers from all walks of life. Get ready to be moved and motivated by Swati Tyagi's relatable BIO, showing that anything is possible with the right mix of tech-savvy and heartfelt care.